Office Correspondence Made Easy

Office Correspondence Made Easy

Master the Basics of Business Letters, Memos, and E-Mail for All Occasions

NEW YORK

Published in the United States by LearningExpress, LLC, New York.

Library of Congress Cataloging-in-Publication Data:
Office correspondence made easy : master the basics of business letters, memos and e-mail for all occasions.—1st ed.
p. cm.
Includes bibliographical references.
ISBN: 978-1-57685-604-8
1. Commercial correspondence. 2. Business communication. I. LearningExpress (Organization)
HF5721.O34 2008
651.7'4—dc22

2008000918

Printed in the United States of America

9 8 7 6 5 4 3 2 1

First Edition

For more information or to place an order, contact LearningExpress at:
55 Broadway
8th Floor
New York, NY 10006

Or visit us at:
www.learnatest.com

Contents

Appendix

Glossary

Introduction

Writing is more important than ever. How often have you heard that said? No doubt teachers repeated that mantra from the time you started to write all the way through high school, college, and even graduate school. Seminars on writing business correspondence (letters, memos, e-mails) proliferate; others offer help with reports, technical papers, requests for proposals (RFPs), and more; you name it they have a course for it. A recent Google search for *business correspondence seminars* yielded "about 1,950,000 hits." Now, we all know there's stuff in there that doesn't count, and lots of repetition; nevertheless, that's a whopping big number!

When it comes to writing on the job, many smart, even well-educated people are afraid to write, believe they can't write, and are looking for help with their business writing. These same people have no problem instant messaging and e-mailing friends. You would think that all that practice gives them a leg up when it comes to writing for work. Apparently, that's not the case.

This lack of confidence comes at a time when writing is more and more what people do each day at work. In fact, many people complain about the lack of face-to-face conversation in the workplace.

All the ubiquitous new devices—from our desktops to our laptops to our cell phones and PDAs—allow us to write (some complain, *demand* that we write) any time, day or night. E-mail isn't writing, you say. Text messaging isn't writing. But of course, they are. And instant messaging (IM), once only for kids, is finding its way into the workplace.

So, why are so many people intimidated when they have to write a letter, a memo, or even a business e-mail? We believe it is because writing, as taught in school, seems to be hard, to lack practical application, to be a series of rules and technical mumbo-jumbo.

WHAT THIS BOOK WILL DO FOR YOU

Because you must write so much, what you write at work has become more important to your career; it is your face to your peers, your boss, your customers, clients, and suppliers. Therefore, the ability to communicate well in writing is an increasingly important part of your evaluations. Although getting a promotion is not determined solely by your writing skill, it does carry great weight.

In business, whatever you write, no matter how abbreviated, must be clear; often it must also be persuasive. This is not really difficult. You do it orally, speaking to friends, family, and colleagues. You can do it in your writing as well. In *Office Correspondence Made Easy*, we've kept the rules to a minimum and presented the essential guidelines in plain English. We have included business-related examples, steps to follow, and plenty of samples that you can refer to whenever you encounter a writing problem.

Office Correspondence Made Easy is composed of two parts.

The first chapter in *Part One: Back to Basics* reviews the differences among letters, memos, and e-mail, and touches on the inroads instant messaging is making and its impact on business writing. We then get the technical issues out of the way in a chapter called *Writing Made Easy: Quick Cures for Common Writing Problems*, in which we cover those problems with grammar and punctuation that sometimes trip up otherwise good writers.

The last chapter in Part One, *A Question of Style: Getting and Keeping Your Readers' Attention*, shows you step by step how to create compelling business correspondence that people will want to read.

In *Part Two: Getting Down to Business*, we provide specific information—including how to approach writing them and what form they should take—for the most frequently written categories of business correspondence:

- announcements
- complaints
- congratulations, get well greetings, and condolences
- credit and collection
- customer correspondence
- the job search
- personnel matters
- references, recommendations, and introductions
- replies
- requests
- thank-you notes

HOW TO USE THIS BOOK

To get the most from *Office Correspondence Made Easy*, we recommend that you start with Part One to refresh your memory and brush up on your skills. You can then move to Part Two and read straight through, or you can consult it whenever you have to write on a particular topic. This will give you ideas to jumpstart your writing.

Pay special attention to the many useful features scattered throughout the text:

- *Tips* providing advice about specific writing issues
- *Did You Know* boxes offering tantalizing tidbits of information that you might not otherwise have known and that can help you not only avoid errors but also make an impression
- *Simply Stated* sidebars that summarize key points along the way

The Appendix and the Glossary give you help with the language of business. In the Appendix, "Say What You Mean; Mean What You Say," you'll find words and phrases that can trip up even the best writers, along with brief explanations and examples of how to use them correctly, as well as a selected list of jargon, euphemisms, and clichés that good business writers should try to edit out of their writing. The Glossary is a quick reference to commonly used business words and phrases that you may encounter or find need for on the job.

Writing can be a rewarding and success-enhancing opportunity. *Office Correspondence Made Easy* provides an entry point into good business writing. The more you write, the easier writing becomes and, therefore, the more comfortable you will be doing it. With comfort comes confidence, then competence, and finally excellence. You can achieve excellence by following the guidelines and building on the samples we provide.

PART one

Back to Basics

CHAPTER ONE

What's the Difference?

Letters and Memos in the Age of E-Mail

The Internet has revolutionized the way we communicate in business as well as in personal life. E-mail is everywhere.

In some companies, the line between e-mail, memos, and even letters has blurred. In some offices, formal memos are practically obsolete unless they are long, in which case they are often attached to an e-mail. Similarly, fewer and fewer businesspeople write letters, even when corresponding with those outside their own organization. Different industries and different companies have different cultures and preferred methods of communicating. It is therefore wise, when you join a new organization, to observe what your colleagues do, and to follow their lead.

When the choice is yours, however, you should be aware of the advantages of choosing one form of communication over another before setting out to write. For this reason, Part One of this book offers a quick review. To guide you further, Part Two points out the pros and cons of using one form or another for a particular type of correspondence.

DELIVER THE LETTERS

For the most part, quality paper with a professionally printed letterhead is used for correspondence. Small and home businesspeople, however, may create their own letterheads—often very effectively—using computer software or templates. Still, many of them select a higher quality paper for letters (usually with matching envelopes) than they do for other things. It makes a good impression.

Letters are a company's face to the outside world: to customers, regulatory agencies, suppliers, and others. Most often, people choose to write a letter when communicating with those outside their company, in order to add a formal yet personal touch to this *external* correspondence. A letter is usually addressed to a single individual (occasionally to a small group) rather than to a large number of people. A letter seems (indeed is) a personal form of communication, although ccs (short for carbon copies—how obsolete is that?—some now call them courtesy copies) are sometimes sent to other people as well.

Some experts suggest that a letter is less official than a memo, but memos (except for something like a Memorandum of Understanding, which is a legal document) were and generally still are not used for external communication.

> **SIMPLY STATED**
>
> Use a letter when
>
> - writing to someone outside your company
> - writing to one person (or to a small group)
> - you want to appear personal and formal
> - you know the reader prefers hard copy over e-mail

Easy Ways to Dress Up Your Letters

Quality paper and a well-designed letterhead for your stationery convey a strong message about your company, so consider investing in them even if you are a freelancer. Letterheads can be printed in one or more colors and they can be embossed, a process that makes the type pop off the page (you can feel it when you run your fingers over it).

However they are printed, most letterheads today include

- company name
- street address
- telephone and fax numbers
- e-mail address

Some letterheads include the company's url (website address).

In the United States, letterhead is $8\frac{1}{2} \times 11$ inches. Most letters are formatted in block style—no paragraph indents—and most use ragged right margins—uneven line lengths (see Figure 1.1) rather than justified (even) right margins, which are more difficult to read (see Figure 1.2). They are single spaced with a double space

company name
street address
city, state zip
telephone number • fax number
e-mail address
url

date

Mr./Ms. full name of recipient
street address
city, state zip

Dear Mr./Ms. last name [or Dear first name (if you know the person)]:

Confirming our conversation, we would like to proceed with upholstering the sectional sofa, in Ultrasuede Ambiance #3694, ivory, and the single chair in black leather, Allure Night. The total price, including tax, will be $9,407.50.

I will let you know when to pick up and deliver the furniture as soon as we confirm when the new office space will be renovated.

Thanks for all your help.

Sincerely,

Jeremy N. Grace
Office Manager

Enclosure [if any]
cc: [if any]

jng/ms [initials of writer/initials of typist; if you typed the letter yourself, use “ms”]

Figure 1.1 Letter Format with Ragged Right Margin

company name
street address
city, state zip
telephone number • fax number
e-mail address
url

date

Mr./Ms. full name of recipient
street address
city, state zip

Dear Mr./Ms. last name [or Dear first name (if you know the person)]:

Confirming our conversation, we would like to proceed with upholstering the sectional sofa in Ultrasuede Ambiance #3694, ivory, and the single chair in black leather, Allure Night. The total price, including tax, will be $9,407.50.

I will let you know when to pick up and deliver the furniture as soon as we confirm when the new office space will be renovated.

Thanks for all your help.

Sincerely,

Jeremy N. Grace
Office Manager

Enclosure [if any]
cc: [if any]

jng/ms [initials of writer/initials of typist; if you typed the letter yourself, use "ms"]

Figure 1.2 Letter Format with Justified Right Margin

between paragraphs. Left and right hand margins are between $1\frac{1}{4}$ and $1\frac{1}{2}$ inches on both sides. As nearly as possible, letters should be centered (top to bottom) on the page.

If a letter runs to a second page, use the same stationery without the letterhead. At the top, insert the name of the recipient, the date, and the page number (see Figure 1.3).

Mr./Ms. full name of recipient	Page 2
date	

Figure 1.3 Continuation Page Format for Letter or Memo

The Parts of a Letter

Although e-letters are gaining ground on the printed variety, letters have an important role in business writing, particularly in company-to-company and company-to-customer communications. Crucial communications and most formal communications are still hard copy letters.

The way a letter is organized is generally the same from company to company:

- letterhead
- date
- inside address
- attention line (if any)
- salutation
- subject line (if any)
- body—the text of the letter
- complimentary closing
- company signature (if used)
- reference initials
- enclosure reminder (if needed)
- cc notation

Don't forget that it is essential to refer to enclosures in the body of the letter and, unless its function or purpose is self-explanatory, make sure the reader knows why you are sending them.

SIMPLY STATED

HELLOS AND GOOD-BYES

If you don't know the recipient, use

- Dear Mr./Ms./Dr. [last name; if not known, use person's title]
- Dear Mrs. [if correspondent indicates this preference]
- Dear [first name, if you know the recipient well, or have been told to use first name, or if the correspondent has used first name in signature]

If you don't know the recipient's name, use

- To Whom It May Concern

The closing you select should be based on the content and formality of the letter, your familiarity with the recipient, and the recipient's level of authority. Acceptable complimentary closings include

- Sincerely (yours)
- Very truly yours
- Best regards (With best regards)
- Best wishes (With best wishes)
- Cordially (yours)
- Respectfully (yours)
- (With) kindest regards

Handwritten Notes

Few of us have the time (or the legible script) to write a letter by hand, but occasionally a well-composed handwritten note sends the strongest, most personal business message, and therefore makes the strongest impact. (Hand-addressing the envelope as well is a good idea.) Thank-you and condolence notes are the most common, but consider a handwritten note for congratulation and other special occasion messages. It practically assures that yours will be noticed.

Appending a handwritten note—just a line or two—to a printed business letter can lend a personal touch. Marketers use this tactic in direct mail advertising to great effect. Another way to personalize your message and get attention is to use a stamp instead of metering your note (or letter)—another advertising technique that's effective in business!

MAKE MINE A MEMO (OR AN E-MEMO)

Memos are *internal* correspondence. Businesses use them to communicate information within the company. In many companies, e-memos have replaced printed memos, entirely or almost entirely. Whatever the mode of distribution, memos are the most frequently used form of business communication. This was true even before the advent of e-mail.

As a rule of thumb, even if you plan to e-mail your memo, it's best to attach it as a Word or WordPerfect document if it is longer than a paragraph or two. Many people still find reading long documents on screen difficult, or they may need to take a printout to a meeting, and, if the systems are not compatible, some e-mails lose format when printed out.

Memos may be addressed to a single person or to an entire company, division, or department. Memos may be written by a boss to subordinates, by colleagues to one another, by subordinates to managers—up, down, and across the chain of command. In addition, people write memos on a subject or to a person's file as a permanent record, for example, of a meeting, a telephone conversation, a performance evaluation, or as a reminder to follow up on something.

Easy Ways to Dress Up Your Memos

Unlike letters, which are usually just text, maybe with some italics or boldfaced type, memos may also contain headings, bullets, white space, and boxes. Memos, too, are printed on $8\frac{1}{2} \times 11''$ paper. Most printed memos look like Figure 1.4 (e-mails look pretty much the same, except for the heading). They let the reader know:

- who got the memo (*to* and *cc*)
- who sent it
- when it was written
- what it is about

Be consistent. If you use titles for one person, use them for all. If you use full names, use everyone's full name, *not* initials for some, full names for others.

The text in a memo should be single spaced. Like a letter, most memos are set in block format.

The Parts of a Memo

Unlike letters, memos do not contain a salutation, although e-mails often do (particularly if the memo itself is in the form of an attachment, and the e-mail becomes a form of cover letter).

MEMORANDUM

To:
CC:
From:
Date:
Subject:

[text]

Figure 1.4 Memo Format

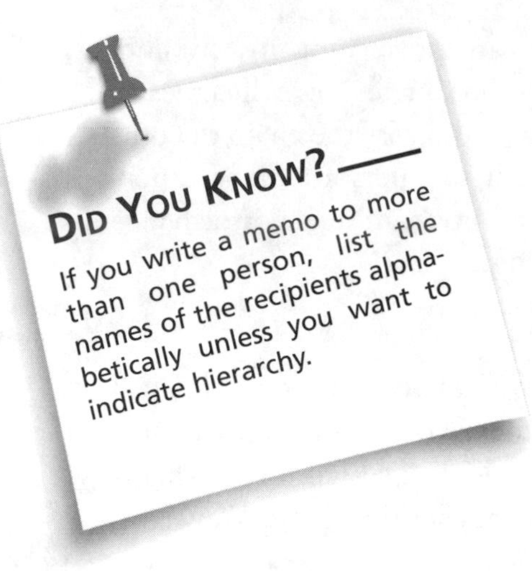

Depending on company style, you may omit titles of senders and recipients, unless the company you work for is so large or so dispersed that not all recipients will recognize every name and know each person's function.

Unlike letters, where subject lines are optional, a memo's subject line is essential; it therefore needs to be informative. Don't just write *Meeting*, write *Meeting to Prepare for Sales Conference*.

Note attachments or enclosures, and, as you would in a letter, refer to the enclosures in the text and explain them, if necessary.

A memo that is going to an entire company can be addressed to *All Personnel* or *Marketing Department Staff* or *Customer Service Department*. Or, if the distribution list is long, making it difficult to list all recipients at the top, you can address the memo to *Distribution* and, at the end, list the names of all the recipients. The same is true for cc lists (see Figure 1.5).

A memo has no place for a written signature, but many people do initial the memo in ink next to their name to ensure its authenticity. Obviously, you can't do this with an e-mail.

MEMORANDUM

To: Kimberly McCarren
CC: Distribution
From: Taylor Schofield
Date: October 12, 200-
Subject: Request for Meeting to Discuss Sales Conference

[text]

cc: Distribution

Mark Elliott	Tim Knight
Graham Fine	Tory Schwartzer
Kathy Jacobs	Melinda Patterson
Cassandra Jones	

Figure 1.5 Memorandum with Distribution List

Computers do crash; if a document is important—whether it's a letter memo or an e-mail—retain a hard copy.

SIMPLY STATED

Use a memo when

- you write to someone inside your organization
- a more formal hard copy might have greater impact than an e-mail
- you want a handwritten signature (initials)
- you know the reader prefers hard copy

YOU'VE GOT MAIL

Those three little words say it all. So much a part of our lives is e-mail that it became the title of a movie. In some businesses, e-mail has replaced hard copy letters and memos. Even where hard copy is used, the number of purposes for which it is used has diminished considerably.

E-mail has the advantage of being fast: literally, in the blink of an eye (if everything is working correctly) an e-mail can land in the recipient's inbox no matter where he or she is. Nothing—except an instant message (IM)—can beat that! E-mail also allows the sender to forward documents, illustrations, photographs, audio, and video in almost any format for viewing as long as the recipient has the program with which to open it.

For short messages, e-mail—even without IM—is a form of conversation. In the time it takes to read and type (and, we hope, give a little thought to the subject), someone can receive and answer it or forward it to others if necessary. What's more, e-mail is portable: It is accessible on laptops, PDAs, and cell phones—in short, it is accessible from almost anywhere at any time.

DID YOU KNOW?

Instant messaging is gaining momentum in the workplace. IM offers many benefits. It's faster than e-mail; used correctly, it's a great customer service tool; and its presence awareness feature lets you see what your correspondent's current status is, and lets others know yours. Many wireless devices and cell phones have an IM feature. But IM has the same risks and the same drawbacks as e-mail and, for now, it only works on a given system, so an AOL customer can't use it to communicate with an MSN customer.

The Pros and Cons of Emoticons

Emotions, made by using keyboard characters to indicate emotion (e.g., :) = ☺), may be okay for writing to friends, but for the workplace, use with caution. In a recent nonscientific survey of a number of business writing books and websites, we found that most experts oppose the use of emoticons (and the companion abbreviations so popular in IM) in business writing, although some seem to be softening their stance.

Our own view is that whether or not you

Did You Know?

LOL (laugh out loud), BRB (be right back), and similar abbreviations (otherwise known as text messaging shorthand, and before that speedwriting) are not in the same category as emoticons. Although they have not yet crept into e-mail, abbreviations are used for instant messaging, cell phones, PDAs, websites, games, and newsgroup postings, in chat rooms, and on blogs. For now, at least, that's where they belong.

use emoticons depends on the context: the nature of the company you work for, the industry you are in, and to whom you are writing and how well you know that person's likes and dislikes. Kristin Byron, an assistant professor of management at Syracuse University's Whitman School of Management, points out that "e-mail generally increases the likelihood of conflict and miscommunication"* and, for this and similar reasons, some people believe that emoticons serve a useful function, even in a business setting.

Still To Be Resolved: The Drawbacks of E-Mail

E-mail has still not replaced hard copy for all people or in all situations. Some people (but they are becoming increasingly rare) simply don't like it. Others say e-mail doesn't have the impact of a physical letter or memo. True, it can't compete with the fine-quality embossed letterhead most companies use. Some people also object that when you print an e-mail, it loses its formatting, which makes it hard to read. While that can be true, more and more systems can send and receive formatted e-mails. Besides, if formatting is a concern, the message can be sent as an attachment, retaining its formatting.

Yet another real problem with e-mail is that it can get lost in the recipient's inbox even more readily than a letter or a memo. People receive so many e-mails—and often so much junk mail, or spam—that an e-mail can easily get lost. A good subject line that lets the recipient know what the e-mail is about will help overcome this problem.

Home businesses and freelancers take note: A clear, easily recognizable e-mail name that lets people know who you are will help overcome the lost-in-the-inbox problem. Cute e-mail addresses are fine for personal e-mail, but for your business, it's wise to choose an address the reader can immediately identify. Otherwise, potential customers may well pass you by. Your own name coupled with the name of your business is your best bet.

---

*Daniel Goleman, "E-Mail Is Easy to Write (and to Misread)" *New York Times*, October 7, 2007.

E-mail is still not the right medium for the most important documents, although, when speed is important, a document can be e-mailed, and hard copy sent by regular mail by way of confirmation. One reason e-mails are not officially recognized is that they can't convey an original signature or initials. But we are getting close: Some programs can insert authenticated signatures into Word and pdf documents.

Another extremely important reason why e-mail has not replaced hard copy is that e-mail is not confidential. Some companies add confidentiality notices to the bottom of every e-mail (see Figure 1.6), but that doesn't stop hackers and other unauthorized persons from viewing your e-mail. Moreover, most of us don't turn off our computers or e-mail programs when we step out of the office for a minute, and, unless you do, there's nothing to stop a snoopy coworker from taking a peek!

SIMPLY STATED

Use e-mail when

- speed is essential, and the telephone isn't appropriate
- short written exchanges are desired
- quick forwarding of messages/documents is needed

Do *not* use e-mail if message/attachments are confidential or the document requires a handwritten signature in order to be valid.

This e-mail message and any attachments contain confidential information from [company name]. If you are not the intended recipient, you are hereby notified that disclosure, printing, copying, distribution, or the taking of any action in reliance on the contents of this electronic information is strictly prohibited. If you have received this e-mail message in error, please immediately notify the sender by reply message and then delete the electronic message and any attachments.

Figure 1.6 Sample Confidentiality Notice

A WORD ABOUT COPIES

Ccs (carbon/courtesy copies) contain the names (in e-mail, the addresses) of recipients of the message. A blind carbon/courtesy copy, or bcc, as its name implies, hides the names of those recipients from all the others.

E-mail specifically, and computers in general, make sending copies, blind or otherwise, easier than it was in the dark ages when copies really were carbon on tissue paper. As a result, the number of recipients of a letter, memo, or e-mail has increased. This breach of etiquette fills the recipients' inbox (electronic or otherwise) with mail they don't need or want and probably won't read. Think twice before deciding who will receive copies of your correspondence; maybe those who write to you will do the same.

CHAPTER **TWO**

Writing Made Easy

Quick Cures for Common Writing Problems

No matter how good your correspondence looks, no matter how fine the stationery, it has to read well. Whether it is a letter, a memo, or an e-mail, it has to get your message across. If it doesn't, there is no point in writing. Therefore, your writing has to be

- clear
- well organized
- easy to understand

It does *not* have to be fancy and high-falutin'; you don't have to use $5 words. On the contrary, in many cases, the simpler your writing the better it is.

Many people see grammar and punctuation as an impossible set of rules they had to memorize in school. Actually, grammar is the skeleton upon which good writing, including correspondence, is hung. It allows us to say what we want to say in a way that won't confuse the reader. The words we use are its sinews, and how we use them gives them vitality.

Not too long ago, there was a best-selling book about punctuation called *Eats, Shoots and Leaves*.* What happens to those four little words when you remove that one little comma? Eats Shoots and Leaves. Clearly, the latter refers to the diet of an animal (in this case a panda); the former refers to what? Could it be a hungry,

---

*Lynne Truss, *Eats, Shoots and Leaves: The Zero Tolerance Approach to Punctuation* (Gotham Books, 2003).

gun-crazed cowboy? (Actually, no; it's the punchline of a joke, but you'll have to read the book!)

For those of you who have forgotten or never learned those dreaded rules, we are going to run through them quickly and try to make them as simple, painless, and nontechnical as we can.

THE POINT ABOUT PUNCTUATION

Punctuation marks are the signs on the highway of clear writing. Some tell us when to slow down, when to pause, when to put on the brakes, and, yes, when to speed up. Others are roadmaps joining one word or sentence to the next and showing us the detours as well as where the exits are.

Road Signs: Commas, Semicolons, and Colons

These punctuation marks are your reader's clue to slow down and take a breath. The comma is the shortest pause, the colon the longest.

Commas

Commas (,) perform several important functions.

- Commas separate two main ideas by using one of these words known as conjunctions: *and*, *but*, *or*, *for*, *nor*, *so*, and *yet*.

A main clause is a complete idea. You could put a period after either of them and each would be a complete sentence.

For example,

> I had to meet with John about the forecasts Mel wanted, *and* I had to recruit someone to compile the data.

could have been:

> I had to meet with John about the forecasts Mel wanted. I had to recruit someone to compile the data.

Using the comma and the word *and* ties the two ideas together, but lets us know that they are two ideas.

- Commas separate introductory material from the main thought.

  On January 6, our new marketing assistant will join the department.

- Commas separate items in a series (words, phrases, clauses).

  I have to meet Crissy, Peter, Elvira, and Edith this afternoon.

- Commas separate interrupters from the main text.

  It is easier, we believe, to write clearly the first time than to have to go back and explain what we meant.

DID YOU KNOW?

When you have a series of things separated by a comma, you can choose to omit the last comma in the series, as in Eats, Shoots and Leaves. It is equally correct—and, we believe, in some cases clearer—to write Eats, Shoots, and Leaves. Whichever you choose, please be consistent.

An interrupter is a word or phrase that can be removed from the sentence without affecting its basic meaning.

- Commas separate some descriptive words from the person, place, or thing they are describing.

  With my bonus, I am going to buy that big, old, overstuffed antique sofa I saw in the shop.

Can you substitute the word *and* for the commas between the adjectives (modifiers) without changing the meaning? Can you reverse the order without changing the logic? Although you could put a comma after overstuffed, it isn't required because it forms a complete thought.

- Commas should go before an *-ing* phrase at the end of a sentence.

  The company saw greater profits, having purchased a new subsidiary.

- Commas are used in dates and addresses.

  January 1, 2008

  New York, NY

Semicolons

The semicolon (;) has only four uses, yet it stymies more writers than most other punctuation. Once you get the hang of it, you'll find semicolons are a worthwhile break.

- Semicolons separate two main ideas when one of the seven little words (the conjunctions *and*, *but*, *or*, *for*, *nor*, *so*, and *yet*) is omitted.

  I had a thousand loose ends to complete before the sales conference; I also had to begin planning the annual convention before I left.

- Semicolons separate two main ideas connected by such words as *accordingly*, *afterwards*, *also*, *consequently*, *however*, *indeed*, *likewise*, *moreover*, *nevertheless*, *nonetheless*, *otherwise*, *similarly*, *so*, *still*, and *therefore*.

  I wanted to begin training the new medical interns immediately; therefore, I asked Jeannette if she would take over my rounds.

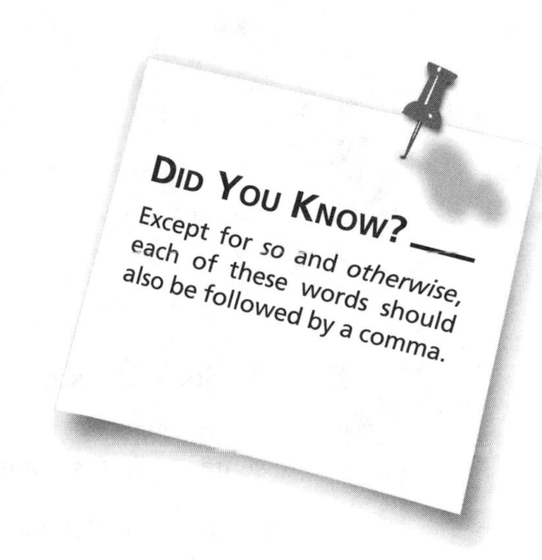

- Semicolons are used when items in a series contain other punctuation, usually commas.

  Marnie Miller, Sales Manager; Frank Messina, COO; and Tony Salieri, CEO, are all in Denver for the industry association get-together.

- Semicolons separate ideas separated by a conjunction when one or both ideas contain other punctuation, usually a comma.

  Marnie Miller, Sales Manager; Frank Messina, COO; and Tony Salieri, CEO, are all in Denver for the industry association get-together; and then they travel on to Bangor to open the new branch office.

Colons

Colons (:) slow the reader down even further.

> **SIMPLY STATED**
>
> COLONS
> - only follow a complete thought
> - are never used after any form of the verb *to be*
> - are never used after a preposition

- Colons are used before a list.

  Petula had myriad tasks to perform before she could leave on vacation: complete performance reviews, write and submit monthly report, submit expense report, and write a follow-up memo for her assistant.

- Colons are used for emphasis; they introduce a "big" thought.

  This is what we have to do: Nail down the costs, cut any fat, and operate lean and mean.

If what follows the colon is a complete sentence, capitalize the first letter.

The Exits: Periods, Question Marks, and Exclamation Points

Periods and question marks require little explanation. Use a period (.) at the end of a complete sentence that is a statement, including an indirect question.

> The Board of Directors wanted to know why the company's expenses were over budget for the quarter.

Use a question mark (?) at the end of a direct question.

> Why were the company's expenses over budget for the quarter?

In formal business writing, do not use a question mark in combination with other punctuation.

Exclamation points (!) are used for emphasis, to express emotion.

> Expenses were down dramatically in the fourth quarter!

They should be used very, very sparingly in formal business writing. In fact, they should be used sparingly in all writing or they lose their impact.

Detours: Dashes and Parentheses

This pair has similar uses. They indicate major changes or afterthoughts.

> It is equally correct—and, we believe, in some cases clearer—to write Eats, Shoots, and Leaves.

A dash may be used—for emphasis—in mid-sentence before items in a series.

> I want to stress growth—increased profits, lower costs, and rising sales—in our annual report.

Dashes are not used in place of a colon before a list.

Did You Know?

Brackets ([/]) indicate additional information or changes within a quotation or parentheses within parentheses.

According to the newspaper report, "He presented his findings to [the Board] at their regular meeting."

(Sarah had read all the material [she wanted so much to be there], but then could not attend the meeting.)

Sometimes, though not always, parentheses can be used in place of a pair of dashes; they also can be used to add information.

> It is equally correct (and, we believe, in some cases clearer) to write *Eats, Shoots, and Leaves* (the words repunctuate the title of an interesting and amusing book by a British author).

Scenic View: Quotation Marks

Quotation marks ("/") raise two issues: (1) when to use them and (2) the thornier question of where to put the other punctuation when you use quotation marks.

Quotation marks are used when

- you are directly repeating what someone said or has written

> According to the newspaper report, "The attendance records at the antiques show were sky high and so were the prices."

- you want to highlight a word, either for clarity or emphasis

  The "patch" of dry land had become a swamp 100 miles wide.

In American English,

- Periods and commas go inside the closing quotation mark.
- Semicolons and colons go outside the closing quotation mark.
- Question marks and exclamation points go inside when they are part of the quoted material and outside when they are not.

Bumps in the Road: Apostrophes and Hyphens

Apostrophes (') are used in contractions, such as *I'm* for *I am*, *you're* for *you are*, and so on.

Contractions are more and more acceptable in business writing, particularly when you want to add a personal touch or make a direct connection with the reader.

They are also used to indicate possessives, where you add *'s* to all words except those ending in *s*, where you only add '. There are some exceptions for proper names. Some say to omit the additional *s* after historical or biblical names; others say to omit it after one-syllable names. Rather than concern yourself with the exceptions, it's safer to use it in all cases.

Hyphens (-) add clarity. Hyphenate

- two words used as a single descriptor of a person, place, or thing unless the descriptor ends in *-ly*; for example, *well-built vehicle*, but *beautifully designed car*
- numbers in combination; that is all numbers between 21 (*twenty-one*) and 99 (*ninety-nine*), but not 616 (*six hundred sixteen*)
- to break words—between syllables—that fall at the end of a typed or typeset line (today, most word-processing programs do this for us)

One-syllable words may not be hyphenated; names should not be hyphenated. Check a dictionary or usage guide for other exceptions.

GETTING THE GIST OF GRAMMAR

If punctuation is the roadmap, grammar is the road along which your correspondence travels. In this section, we're going to look at some of the things that cause many writers problems, and show how to solve them.

Agreement: Subject-Verb Agreement

Continuing with our road metaphor, in simple terms, the subject (noun or pronoun) is the driver and the verb is the vehicle. There can be one driver or there can be many. When there is one driver, the form of vehicle it uses is also singular.

> *He is* at the meeting.

When there are multiple drivers, the vehicle is plural.

> *They are* at the meeting.
>
> *John and his bosses are* at the meeting.

When there are two subjects, one of which is singular and the other plural, the verb agrees with the subject closest to it.

> *John or his bosses are* at the meeting.
>
> *His bosses or John is* at the meeting.

When the subject (multiple drivers) comes mid-sentence, the rule still applies.

> At the meeting *are John and his bosses*.

Either/or and *neither/nor* work in the same fashion: The verb agrees with the nearer subject.

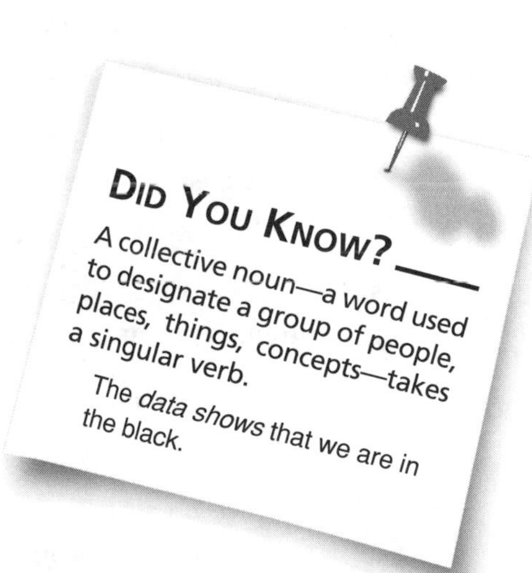

The Agreement Conundrum: Indefinite Pronouns and Agreement

Indefinite pronouns such as *everybody*, *anybody*, *somebody*, *all*, *each*, *every*, *some*, *none*, *one*, *several*, and *others* are singular and, therefore, take singular verbs.

> *Each of us is* going to the meeting.

Did You Know?

Some experts prefer sprinkling *his* or *her* interchangeably throughout the document, but we find this can sometimes be confusing or off-putting.

So far, so good, but now what do you do?

Each of us is going to the meeting in his/her/their car.

Once, you would automatically have answered, in *his* car, but today's writers strive to avoid sexist language. You could say *his or her* or *her or his*, but that can get awkward after a while. Or you could say *their*, which is what most writers do these days, as it is increasingly accepted as correct. Our preference is, whenever possible without going through contortions, to reword the sentence.

We are going by car to the meeting and taking our own cars.

Not the most elegant solution, but it works.

The choice is yours.

The Problem with Pronouns: Reference, Case, and the "Self" Pronouns

It is easy to use a pronoun and forget that the reader may not know what subject (noun) the pronoun is representing. Consider the following sentences.

Instant messaging is a boon to the customer service business. *It* has expanded exponentially in the past five years.

Which has expanded exponentially: instant messaging or the customer service business? You can clarify the sentences by rewording them. In this instance, one long sentence is clearer that two short ones.

Instant messaging, which has grown exponentially in the past five years, is a boon to the customer service business.

By *case*, we mean the form of the pronoun: *I*, *we*, *he*, *she*, *you*, or *they* (subjective case) is used when the pronoun is the subject of the sentence, and *me*, *us*, *him*, *her*, *you*, or *them* (objective case) is used when the pronoun is the object of the sentence. These pronouns rarely give us problems when used alone, but put two of them together and speakers and writers are often lost. When in doubt, test yourself.

Between you and me, this business trip is going to be a disaster.

Would you say *between I*? No. Therefore, *between you and I* would be incorrect.

She and I went on this business trip together, and it was a disaster.

Here, you could delete either *she* or *I* and the sentence would be correct, but what if you said *she and me*? *Me went* is obviously wrong. Try substituting *her and I*. Does that work? *Her went?* It doesn't work.

> Thank you so much for including Coral, Penelope and *I* in your group.

Thank you so much for including *I*? I think not; choose *me* instead. Or consider substituting *us*.

You'll always get case right if you *never* mix subjective pronouns (or nouns) with objective pronouns (or nouns).

Technically, the "self" pronouns fall into two categories: reflexive and intensive pronouns. They include *myself*, *yourself*, *ourselves*, *themselves*, and so on. Their purpose is to

- refer to the preceding noun or pronoun
- emphasize the preceding noun or pronoun

They are never a substitute for the noun or pronoun. Thus,

> *Myself* cannot go to the office. (incorrect)

but

> I can go to the office by *myself*. (correct, reflexive use)

and

> I *myself* can go to the office. (correct, intensive use)

The Worst Pronouns of All: *Who* and *Whom*

They seem innocuous at first. *Who* is the subject and *whom* is the object of the sentence or clause.

> Nick Kazan, *who* is president of the company, is retiring in March.
>
> Nick Kazan, *whom* we greatly admire, is retiring as president of the company in March.
>
> *Who* is running the ad campaign?
>
> With *whom* have you discussed running the ad campaign?

There are rules, but when in doubt, the easiest way to get it right is to rephrase the sentence or clause.

> With *who/whom* have you discussed the ad campaign?

Rephrased

> You are going to discuss the ad campaign with he/him?

Clearly, you would say *with him*; therefore, *whom* is the correct choice.

Another clue is the preposition, which tells you to go with *whom* because it is the object of the sentence.

> Nick Kazan, *who/whom* is president of the company, is retiring in March.

Rephrase the clause

> He/him is president of the company.

Obviously, *he*; therefore, *who* is the correct choice.

Spreading Confusion

When a sentence is poorly constructed, it may cause confusion, mistakes, and sometimes a good belly laugh.

> Relieved of your job responsibilities, your home should be your haven.

Who was relieved? As written, it is *your home*. Clearly, that is not what the writer means. All becomes clear when you rephrase the sentence.

> When Michael was relieved of his job responsibilities, his home became his haven.

Technically, the error is that the modifier in the first sentence is modifying *your home*, which is the subject of that sentence. To correct the error, find the subject and place the modifier as close to it as possible.

Sentences beginning with *-ing* phrases frequently lead to confusion.

> Running the copier, papers flew wildly into the air.

Papers weren't running the copier, were they? Again, you can easily repair this error by stating the real subject of the sentence.

As Sarah was running the copier, the papers flew wildly into the air.

Practically, this is a difficult error to detect because we know what we mean; we know that *your* is really Michael, but will your reader? We know that Sarah was running the copier, but will your reader? Of course not! Try to read what you write as if you knew nothing about the subject. It can open your eyes to errors you might otherwise miss.

Another common error that may throw your readers occurs when we don't list each thing in the same way or introduce phrases in the same way. This can happen in a sentence or in a list. To avoid confusion, we want to create *parallel construction*.

The speaker talked about these trends:

- unemployment
- pay equity
- taking vacation pay in lieu of time off

You can fix this in one of two ways:

The speaker talked about these trends:

- unemployment
- pay equity
- vacation pay in lieu of time off

or, in a more informative way, like this:

The speaker talked about these trends:

- rising unemployment costs
- decreasing pay equity
- taking vacation pay in lieu of time off

Either one of these can be turned into a sentence:

The speaker talked about these trends: rising unemployment costs, decreasing pay equity, and taking vacation pay in lieu of time off.

CHAPTER THREE

A Question of Style

Getting and Keeping Your Readers' Attention

Okay, we have finally arrived at the 64,000-dollar question. We've covered the mechanics: differences among letters, memos, and e-mails, and when to use which (and we have seen how the gap among them is closing). We've talked about the dreaded road-blocks of grammar and punctuation. What we haven't talked about is what to say and how to say it best.

Some people seem to have no problems writing just about anything; other people find writing torture; others just don't seem to care. One of the skills that helps us get ahead and stay ahead is communication. And communication takes two forms: oral and written. Those who go furthest in the work world usually master both.

That doesn't mean you have to be an orator like John F. Kennedy or Martin Luther King. Nor does it mean you have to be Hemingway. It does mean that you have to follow these steps:

1. get your readers' attention
2. keep your readers' attention
3. provide your readers with the information they need
4. make your point clearly (and often succinctly)

You may also have to

5. persuade your readers to act

Until you get to point five, your primary reason for writing is to *provide information*—and many letters, memos, and e-mails are written for just that purpose. Once you get to five—you are probably writing a memo or a letter—you want to *motivate your readers to act*. That action could be on your behalf, as when you ask for a reference; it could also be on behalf of the company, department, or even the readers' own behalf.

Sometimes a straightforward request is all that it takes to persuade your reader to do something; sometimes you may make recommendations, present alternatives, provide the reasons for the action, or demonstrate that the action will be advantageous to the person or the organization.

To motivate your audience, you need to tell them three basic things:

1. *why* you are writing
2. *what* you want them to do
3. *why* they should do it

Frequently, you must tell them by *when* they should do it and, sometimes, *where* it is to be done.

GETTING AND KEEPING ATTENTION

Before you can motivate, you must make sure that the person or persons receiving your correspondence will read it. There several ways you can accomplish this.

Entice Your Reader with a Meaningful Subject Line

Most letters don't contain a subject line, but memos and e-mails do. The subject line alone (unless you happen to be the boss) may make the difference between whether your memo is read (and, in the case of an e-mail, even whether it is opened) or not. Mind you, it doesn't have to be cute or clever—in fact, it probably should not be; but it should motivate (there's that word again) the reader to open the e-mail. That means be specific. Compare these

Confirming	Confirming guest list—lunch Tuesday
Meeting with JKL	Agenda for meeting with JKL
Monthly reports	Deadline change for monthly reports

Write to Your Reader

You have probably heard this phrase before. It's a worthwhile piece of advice and worth repeating. In fact, you should write to your reader even when you are writing to a group. By writing to your reader (as we do in this book), you *include* the reader and make your reader part of (even a participant in) whatever it is you are writing about. This is particularly useful when you are writing to persuade an individual or a group to take action.

To know whom you are writing to, you need to determine what the reader knows and doesn't know, and what the reader *needs* to know and *doesn't* need to know (the president of the company may not need the same level of detail as the person who will implement the task, for example). You'll also need to bear in mind what role the reader will play and why he or she will want to play it (more about this later in the chapter).

Be Personal: Involve Your Audience

Using pronouns (*you*, *we*, *I*, *us*, *ours*, *me*, *yours*) is the easiest way to embrace your reader. Many writers use the person's name in the body of their correspondence. Direct mail letters use this technique—computers make it easy—that may be why it sounds false to your ears.

> Maryann, this is an excellent opportunity to join the Professional Women's Association.

DID YOU KNOW?

This is even truer as businesses globalize. Many people to whom we write nowadays (and this is true both internally and externally) do not speak English as their first language. Colloquialisms, idioms, jargon, and most especially humor may fly over your readers' heads (and in some cases may unwittingly give offense). Remember, too, greater formality is expected outside the United States as well as in certain industries within the United States.

Some writers can pull this technique off; they know just how often to use a name and where to use it; they also seem to have a sixth sense for whom among their readers will respond positively and who won't. If you think you are one of those, you can try it. For the rest, we recommend against it, and instead suggest you write

> This is an excellent opportunity for *you* to join the Professional Women's Association.

Either of these is infinitely preferable to

> This is an excellent opportunity for one to join the Professional Women's Association.

Choose the Level of Formality That Suits Your Audience

Some say letters are formal, memos are official, and e-mails are casual (some say business e-mails are sometimes too casual). As a rule of thumb, that's true and you won't go wrong with it.

However, there is another—sometimes more important—criterion, which is to consider to whom you are writing.

In any correspondence, the tone—which includes the words you choose—and the level of formality should suit the audience. Be careful about how casual you wish to be, even in an e-mail to someone in business with whom you may also be friends. Correspondence is copied and passed around with great ease; all it takes for an e-mail to be forwarded is a slip of the finger.

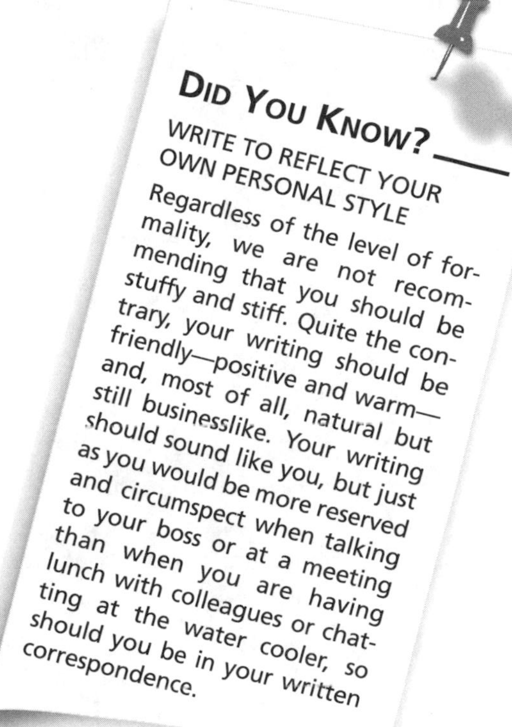

Coming across as arrogant and self-serving is a sure way to turn your readers off, even if they do agree with your point of view.

SIMPLY STATED

Dos and don'ts of getting and keeping attention:

- Do write compelling subject lines for memos and e-mails.
- Do write to your reader.
  - Be personal—use personal pronouns.
  - Choose a level of formality to suit your audience.
- Do be yourself.
  - Be friendly, positive, and natural.
  - Be businesslike.
- Don't be stuffy and stiff.
- Don't sound arrogant or self-serving.

THINK BEFORE YOU WRITE

Whether you are writing to provide information or writing to persuade, there are some key things to consider. Depending upon your message's importance, its complexity, and the amount of time you have to write, your approach will vary considerably.

Still, no matter what it is you are writing—even if it is something as simple as an e-mail confirming an appointment—pause and give what you are going to say some thought. The time you spend up front will ultimately save you time, and it may prevent you and your reader from being inconvenienced.

Look at the e-mail in Figure 3.1. Is anything wrong with it? It's brief; it's to the point. It's fine. Right? Wrong!

To: Gail Morrison
From: Noreen MacPherson
Date: Sat 10/13/07 11:37 A.M.
Subject: Confirming Lunch Date

See you on Tuesday.

Figure 3.1 E-Mail Confirmation (Incorrect)

Most business e-mails contain some sort of greeting, if only the name of a person with whom you correspond frequently. Many e-mails don't have a formal closing, but they should contain a signature, if only your first name, which, again, is fine if you are writing to someone with whom you frequently correspond.

More important, though, the e-mail fails to convey important information: the time, the date (yes, the writer said Tuesday, but *which* Tuesday?—mistakes can and do happen), and the name of the restaurant or meeting place and its address (yes; if it is well known to both parties, perhaps the address can be omitted).

Not including this information makes it more difficult for the recipient; putting it in one place is a simple courtesy and demonstrates that you consider your appointment important.

Crafting Your Message

It is often a good idea, especially in an e-mail, but also in letters and memos, to focus on one idea, particularly if it is a complicated idea. It is also a good idea to ask yourself these six questions before putting fingers to keyboard:

1. What is my goal?
2. What is (are) my readers' goal(s)?
3. What am I going to recommend to my readers?
4. How will I support my position?
5. What action(s) am I going to request?
6. What are the next steps/deadlines?

These questions serve two purposes: (1) They organize your thoughts and (2) they serve as the basis of a formal or informal outline of your correspondence (more about that later in this chapter). Whether or not you are able to answer these questions should tell you whether you should be writing this now or at all. The lack of a good answer may tell you it is not a good idea or that you haven't done enough work on it and need to get back to the drawing board.

State Your Goal: Your Reason for Writing

Often your readers will recognize your goal from the subject line, if it's a memo or e-mail. In a letter, state your goal in the first sentence or, at the latest, in the first paragraph. It is frequently a good idea to restate or expand on your purpose for writing in the first sentence of a memo or e-mail.

> I am applying to Wharton for an MBA, and a letter of recommendation from you would greatly help my chances for acceptance.

State Your Readers' Goal: Their Reason for Being Interested

This can be harder, as in the case of the reference request, but even when there is no apparent advantage to the writer, you often can find one.

> I am applying to Wharton for an MBA, and a letter of recommendation from you would greatly help my chances for acceptance. I believe an MBA in finance will significantly enhance my value to the Mergers and Acquisitions Department here at William Barnum & Co.

Identify why your goals and your readers' goals complement one another or coincide and—implicitly or explicitly—make them the centerpiece of your memo.

> For many years, the Chicago branch has been operating with one hand tied behind its back. Its staff is small and its office shabby. Renovating it and adding three additional people, two salespeople and one assistant, would let us hit the ground running as we launch our new ad blitz. It will also reduce, if not eliminate, the need for support the New York office has had to provide.

State Your Recommendation

Sometimes, as in the Wharton example on the previous page, your recommendation is included in your statement of goals. In other instances, you must make your recommendation clear.

> It is to our advantage to launch the ad campaign before the back-to-school season when we will be competing against much bigger companies with larger budgets. In addition, ads are less expensive in July and August.

Support Your Position

Figures are often the best way to support your position. They are especially helpful if you believe you must also counter anticipated objections. In the previous ad example, you might consider adding

> Although conventional wisdom suggests waiting until September, when people are no longer in "summer mode," several blockbuster products—Carry-all Lunchboxes, $1 million; Nice 'n Neat Notebooks, $3.5 million; and Slicker Slickers, over $10 million, all in their first quarter—were launched in this fashion by small companies, who achieved big market share.

At other times, what you are suggesting may not have immediate or direct financial benefit, so you need to look elsewhere to support your position.

DID YOU KNOW?

If you don't have the facts to support your position, you shouldn't be writing until you do. Do your research first; it will pay off in the positive results and good feedback you get.

> Ethics in business, it is said, has a negative effect on the bottom line, but consider these two items:
>
> 1. Would you rather do business with a company that has a reputation for unethical conduct or ethical conduct? Research shows that short term, it may cost more, but long term, it pays off.
> 2. Would you rather work for an ethical or an unethical company? Studies show that employers with ethical reputations recruit and keep the best.

Request Actions, If Any, to Be Taken

Some communications are simply informational; in others, you'll be suggesting actions that are required to move the recommendation forward. Bulleted or numbered lists (as shown in the preceding example) are useful here.

> I recommend that we do an analysis to determine
>
> - how much the new filing system would cost to purchase
> - how much it would cost to implement
> - how we could transition to it with the least amount of disruption

Recommend Next Steps and/or Deadlines

> To get this project started, I suggest each department head appoint one person to investigate what the impact of making the transition to the new filing system would be on each department, and what, if anything, would be gained from it. As they conduct their studies, the business managers of each department should evaluate the cost to their departments.
>
> These reports and should be completed by June 17 and should be distributed to all department heads as well as the COO. With this data in hand, we should meet again no later than June 30 to evaluate what the savings, if any, would be in actual dollars as well as time spent on this function, and make a go/no-go decision.
>
> I will check everyone's calendar and e-mail each participant with a firm date for the meeting.

Be Brief

With all that you do, you may ask, how can any but the most mundane correspondence be brief? Well, brief is a relative term, but if you organize what you have to say, you'll be able to say it the shortest possible way that will get your message across.

As a rule, letters and memos should not be longer than two pages and an e-mail not more that several paragraphs (if an e-mail is longer, consider sending it as an attachment).

In addition, as you organize your thoughts, you may discover that you are really addressing more than one topic. The topics may relate to one another, it is true; and there are times when there is no way to pull the strands apart. But more often than not, you can easily deal with several topics if you organize your thoughts first.

Be Clear

Some say sentences should be short for readability and paragraphs should be short to allow white space on the page. Some even say short words are best. There are occasions when this is true. We prefer the idea of alternating—some long, some short—to make your writing more interesting. (Warning: Don't do this by rote; alternating every other one can become boring, too.)

The same is true of the words you use. Don't use long words or jargon in order to show off; more often than not, they will result in confusion, and no one will be impressed. On the other hand, if you need to use long words or jargon that some of your readers may not understand, clarify them by their context or define them.

The bottom line: Choose words and sentences that best say what you need to say. Don't be vague or qualify each word with a wishy-washy modifier. Be direct. Omit unnecessary words that slow the reader down. Structure paragraphs around one main point; the rest of the sentences in that paragraph should reinforce that point, not introduce a new thought. Topic sentences are guideposts for you as you write and for your audience as they read. In building a house, you pile one brick on another; similarly, in correspondence, you set one word after another to form a sentence. You set one sentence after another to form a paragraph. Before you know it you have an e-mail, a memo, or a letter.

THE WRITING PROCESS

There are several steps to the writing process:

- outlining/planning
- drafting/writing
- editing/rewriting

Working Your Plan

Earlier in this chapter, we touched on the first step, outlining/planning, in our discussion of the six questions to ask yourself before you write. Those six questions (page 30) are the basis for your plan. Everything you write should be planned, but not everything you write needs to be planned with the same level of detail.

Take Figure 3.2, for example. Did you need a written outline? The answer is definitely not. Did you even have to ask yourself the six questions? Definitely not.

To: Gail Morrison
From: Noreen MacPherson
Date: Sat 10/13/07 11:37 A.M.
Subject: Confirming Lunch Date

Dear Gail,
I am looking forward to seeing you on Tuesday, October 16, at Chez Moi Bistro, 236 Park Avenue South, at 12:30. The reservation is in my name.
Best regards,
Noreen

Figure 3.2 E-Mail Confirmation (Correct)

What you did have to do was not forget any of the vital information. For this, you might quickly ask yourself

- *who* (did anyone else need this information?)
- *what* (confirm lunch date)
- *when* (date and time)
- *where* (name and address)
- *why* (not needed, as you are confirming, *not* arranging the date)

For a detailed letter or memo, the six points are essential guideposts.

Should you write down your outline, or could you just bear it in mind? Many experts advocate a written—although not necessarily formal—outline whenever you write. Given how much we have to write, and all the constraints on our time, an outline is a benefit when writing about something complex—it gives you a roadmap to follow—but not necessary for more routine correspondence.

If you are just starting a job or familiarizing yourself in a new area, outlining even routine correspondence is a good idea. After time, you will gain facility and some of your correspondence will become second nature (but, we hope, never rote).

DID YOU KNOW?

Writing is a very personal process. Some people work best from very detailed outlines; others outline loosely and let creativity, serendipity, and experience fill in the details. The key word here is *experience*: no matter how creative you are, as a beginner you should write with a plan.

Getting It Down: The First Draft

Once you have a plan, you'll find that writing the first draft goes much faster. This is especially true if you have a detailed outline. Some writers find that writing the easy parts first, the harder parts next, and the introductory material last works best for them. Some move back and forth among sections; some edit as they go (and then reedit when they have finished); others write their first draft straight through without rereading, editing, or worrying about grammar, punctuation, and spelling.

The important thing here is that this is a *draft*, not the final product. Therefore, what counts at this stage is whatever gets your juices flowing and gets the words down on paper.

The Proof Is in the Reading: Editing Your Words

If you write directly from an outline and follow it precisely, you may find that the editing process is nothing more than correcting grammar and spelling, with the occasional adjustment of tone.

If you don't work from a detailed outline, the editing process is much more involved. In addition to checking for grammar, spelling, and tone, you'll need to ask yourself

- Did you miss anything—for example, a key point or an important piece of information?
- Are your points logically sequenced and presented logically?
- Have you repeated yourself?
- Have you presented only one key idea in each paragraph?

DID YOU KNOW?

The lead-in to the joke asks, Do you want the good news or the bad news? The rule in business writing is good news first; bad news last. When delivering bad news, first put it in context, but don't bury it.

Even when you work from a detailed outline, it is a good idea to ask yourself these questions.

If you have time—and you should allow time to write important correspondence—put it aside, sleep on it overnight, and come back to it fresh the next day (if possible). Even if you have only a short amount of time, put what you have written aside, do something else, and come back to it with fresh eyes. Even this small amount of time will give you perspective and allow you catch things you might otherwise miss.

However you write and edit, *do not rely* on grammar and spell checkers. They can help, but they can't pick up some types of errors, and, all too often, they are incorrect. For example, my grammar checker tells me to add a comma after the word *however* at the beginning of this tip. That's incorrect; in this context, *however* means *no matter how*, and no comma is needed; in fact, it would be wrong.

DID YOU KNOW?

Taking a break from what you have written is doubly, even triply important when anger or emotion are driving what you say. The first rule, of course, is: Don't write when you are angry or emotional. If you do, set aside what you've written, don't look at it for a while—preferably a day or two—and then decide (1) if you want to send it at all, and (2) if the answer is yes, ask yourself, is this how I want to say it? The answer to that is probably no. In either case, shred or delete all copies; you don't want this falling into the wrong hands!

PART two

Getting Down to Business

CHAPTER **FOUR**

Announcements

Now Hear This!

Whatever your business, you are always announcing something—to staff as well as to customers, vendors, partners, the media, and others. Announcements span a wide range of subjects:

- a change in policy or price
- a change in terms of sale
- a clarification
- a special offer
- an opening or closing
- a new product
- a new hire
- a promotion
- a retirement
- a termination
- and many more

Sometimes announcements convey good news; at other times, the news may not be what the recipient wants to hear. In either case, announcements convey important information that the recipient needs to know or that you want the recipient to know.

For this reason, effective announcements focus on a single piece of information and, with a few exceptions, are direct, clear, and concise.

SIMPLY STATED

- Make your message clear in the first paragraph.
- Inform readers whether or not action is required.
- Ensure deadlines are clearly stated.
- Remember: Shorter is better.

Announcements these days take many forms: cards, letters, e-mails, and memos. They may even take the form of a classified ad in a newspaper or a trade magazine. Most announcements cover only one topic because their function is to convey an important piece of information. That is why announcements need to be clear, to the point, and easy to understand.

Most often, announcements—whether internal or external—contain time-sensitive information. What's the point of announcing a personnel change after the person has been with the company or in a new position for a month or two? What would happen if you announced a price change a week after it actually took effect? On the other hand, you don't want to announce a grand opening or a sale too far in advance of the event; people may forget about it, or you will lose the sense of excitement you hope the event will generate.

If it's a big event, and you must announce early, consider a *save the date* before the official announcement or invitation goes out, and/or a reminder as the date draws near. An RSVP also adds a note of importance.

ANNOUNCEMENTS TO THE OUTSIDE WORLD

While some companies use e-mail to communicate with customers, partners, and others outside the company, a letter lends more weight to the message and is less likely to get lost in your recipients' inbox. We recommend that if what you are announcing is important—and it usually is—a letter is the best way to send that message.

Announcing a New Hire to Customers

Here, too, we prefer a letter to an e-mail or a memo because it is a communication that is going to people outside the organization and a letter's formality gives the announcement a little more weight and importance.

Dear Joe,

I am proud to introduce Jonah Jacobs, our new Vice President of Sales. He brings with him a wealth of experience in all aspects of the publishing industry.

As you may know, Jonah began his publishing career as a stock clerk in the Boston Book Emporium while still an undergraduate at MIT. He went on to earn an MBA from Harvard Business School in 1998, still supporting himself at BBE, where he'd risen to night and weekend manager.

After graduation, Jonah joined Jones & Co., Booksellers, as assistant manager and rose to manager two years later. With the knowledge and perspective he gained on the retail side, he joined Morris & Mann Publishing Company as their New England sales representative, ultimately moving up to Regional Sales Manager for the northeast.

His intimate understanding of the challenges facing our industry today makes him the ideal person for the job. Please join us in welcoming him, and, if you are attending BEA, please stop by our booth #123-72 and say hello. I'm looking forward to seeing you there.

Best regards,

Announcing a Price Change

Price changes don't fall into the good news category, but the information is vitally important to your customer and your company. There is no way to soften the blow, so don't fudge or hedge, just tell your readers what they need to know.

If you are changing the price on only one item, consider putting it on card stock, but mail it in an envelope. Postcards are often overlooked in the large quantities of mail businesspeople receive each day.

Did You Know?

Appearance counts. You don't want an important message to end up in the circular file. Announcements should not look like a form letter or junk mail. Computers let you easily customize your message with the recipient's name or a personal greeting. When the list is too long to personalize, your message can still look great—quality paper and attractive design will catch the eye and get it opened . . . and read!

IMPORTANT ANNOUNCEMENT

Effective June 17, the price of Better Batter will be:

1–5 cases	$89.52/case
6–10 cases	$83.75/case
11 or more cases	$76.32/case

Juanita Ruiz
Product Manager
Better Batter Division
B & B Baking, Inc.

DID YOU KNOW?

In some industries, classified ads in trade publications are used to announce price changes, changes in discount or returns policies, and other essential customer information. The ad would contain the same information as a postcard except without the name and title of the sender (just the corporate name).

Announcing a New Product

Sometimes you need to broadcast information to a very large number of people. In such cases, it would be costly and time consuming to personalize each letter, and "Dear Customer" may be your only option.

Dear Customer,

Husky Power Mower has partnered with Swifty Snow Blower and come up with an attachment to your mower that will take the broken back out of snow removal.

If you're like most many of us, you've been shoveling for years, and when the inches grew into feet you might even have bribed the kids to lend a hand. Maybe you've even hired a snow removal company and waited for hours, unable to leave your driveway and get to the office.

An aching back from shoveling can now become a thing of the past. With the Husky/Swifty snow blower attached to your mower, you'll be able to plow a 30-foot driveway in 15 minutes and be out on the road or relaxing by the fire without a bad back or hours of toe tapping waiting for plow to show up.

Even better is the Husky/Swifty's low price of $750, and our convenient 12-month, no-interest payment plan. Come in to any of our four convenient locations for a test drive. We know you'll be convinced.

Best regards,

Stan Johnson
Vice President
Mowers and Snowplows Division

Announcing a Special Offer

Dear Customer,

To say thank you to all our wonderful customers and to celebrate 50 years in the Fairfield community, Fairfield Salon and Spa will be offering a free manicure with every facial. We look forward to seeing you in March and to serving the community for another 50 years!

Your Friends,

John, Sally, Sara, and Tom

Announcing a Change in Terms of Sale

Dear Customer:

Effective November 3, we will require a 50% deposit on orders for all custom draperies, shades, and blinds. The balance will be due on installation. We regret any inconvenience this change may cause our loyal customers; however, modifications in our vendors' terms have necessitated this change. Thank you for your cooperation.

Sara and Ted Miller
Owners
Dorchester Window Decorations

MANAGEMENT AND PERSONNEL CHANGES

These days, internal announcements such as those that follow are sent either as an e-mail or as a printed memo. They may be distributed companywide or to a specific department or departments.

> **SIMPLY STATED**
>
> Consider your audience. Ask yourself:
>
> - Why am I sending this announcement?
> - Who really needs the information?
>
> Then, send it only to those who need it.

Announcing a Promotion

Subject: Promotion

Effective immediately, Robin Paula has been named National Executive Chef. Robin brings years of experience in the culinary industry to her new position.

She joined Fine Food Faster after receiving a degree from the Culinary Institute of America, and working in five-star restaurants in New York, New Jersey, and Florida. She joined our team at FFF as Executive Chef for the Eastern Region, a challenging position to which she has brought creativity, ingenuity, and dedication for the past three years. Among her successes was the design and implementation of our Middle Eastern menu and the redesign of the Newark kitchen, which increased both productivity and quality.

In her new position, Robin will be responsible for coordinating the operations of the six regional kitchens, menu planning, and purchasing. Under her guidance, the other kitchens throughout the company will be redesigned to meet the needs of our continually growing list of clients.

Please join me in congratulating Robin on a job well done and wishing her success as she faces even greater challenges.

Announcing a Retirement

Subject: Retirement

Rose Brown will be retiring on September 20 after 30 years with Green & Co. Moved by Hurricane Katrina's recent devastation, she has decided to leave us to face new challenges volunteering with Habitat for Humanity in New Orleans.

Rose joined us as an administrative assistant when she was just out of college and we were a small start-up. As we grew—in no small measure as a result of her efforts—she moved into various positions: first as copywriter, then as advertising manager, next as Vice President for Marketing, and then as Executive VP for Sales and Marketing.

Among her many accomplishments are the launch of Burbling Baby, now our most popular doll, and the repositioning of Squishy

Fishy, moving it from a one-fish bath toy to a major brand with over 50 fish and numerous sea creatures to its credit. Rose was also a major force behind the TV/movie licensing program, which is now the largest single source of both revenue and profit.

We will miss Rose's can-do attitude, enormous creativity, and enthusiasm, and know she will bring the same qualities to Habitat. Please help us send Rose off in style with a dinner at J & J's Steak and Seafood on Tuesday, September 15, and join me in extending a warm farewell and congratulations.

Announcing a Termination

These are among the most difficult announcements. There are legal as well as personal issues involved. For this reason, less is more in announcing a termination.

Subject: Personnel Change

Effective immediately, Paul Cooper will be leaving the firm to pursue other interests. Until we hire someone as Production Director, Jesse Offenbach will be responsible for the widget group and Debra Engle will oversee the nuts and bolts section.

Please join me in extending Paul your best wishes in future endeavors.

POLICY AND PROCEDURE CHANGES

Whether you are announcing a new company policy or a change in one, it is critical that these announcements mean what they say and say what they mean because people will base important decisions on them. Confusion can lead to chaos, and, in some instances, can have legal ramifications.

Subject: Vacation and Holiday Schedule for the Coming Year

The New Year is just around the corner, and it's time to make plans for the coming year. Next year, the office will be closed for the following holidays:

Monday and Tuesday, December 31 and January 1—New Year's Day
Monday, January 21—Birthday of Martin Luther King, Jr.
Monday, February 18—Presidents' Day
Monday, May 26—Memorial Day

Friday, July 4—Independence Day
Monday, September 1—Labor Day
Monday, October 13—Columbus Day
Thursday and Friday, November 27 and 28—Thanksgiving Day
Thursday and Friday, December 25 and 26—Christmas Day

In addition, each employee may take up to three personal days to use at his or her discretion.

Our vacation policy has not changed. In the coming year, each employee is entitled to:

year 1–5: 2 weeks (for those with less than one year's service, vacation time will be prorated)
year 6–10: 3 weeks
year 10–15: 4 weeks
year 15+: 5 weeks

Department heads must approve vacation schedules. We will make every effort to accommodate your desired vacation time. In order to ensure that each department is properly covered and schedules are met, please let your department head know your plans as far in advance as possible. In the event of a scheduling conflict, your manager's decision will be based on date of notification and workflow.

If you have any questions relating to vacation or holidays, please contact your department head or human resources manager.

Announcing a Clarification

Dear Customer,

Subject: Returns Policy

In the guidelines we sent for our new returns policy that went into effect on July 16, the guidelines for returning Model X3-725 were omitted. As a result, we will honor the old policy through the end of August and the new policy will go into effect on September 1.

Beginning September 1, we will accept returns on Model X3-725 for six months from date of purchase. All returns will be authorized on written request, which should include invoice number. A prepaid return authorization label will then be sent to you.

We regret any inconvenience this omission caused.

Sincerely,

SPECIAL EVENTS

A special event can range from a holiday party for staff or customers to the grand opening of a new location.

Subject: Holiday Party

That time of year has rolled around once again, and with great pleasure we invite you and one guest to join us for dinner and dancing at our annual holiday celebration.

Friday, December 15
7 P.M. to midnight
Grand Ballroom, Court Street Plaza Hotel

We've had a good year and there is much to celebrate!

Announcing a New Office or Another Location

The opening of a new store or office could take the form of a letter or an invitation such as this:

Picturesque Pools

Please join us on
Tuesday, July 15, 5 P.M. to 8:30 P.M.
to celebrate the grand opening of our newest store
at
31327 San Fernando Valley Drive

Wine and cheese will be served and each guest will receive a special Picturesque Pools Package, with valuable coupons for big discounts on accessories.

CHAPTER **FIVE**

Complaints

Keep It Civil; See Results

As in your personal life, things can go wrong in your business life. Sometimes you have to make a complaint, or apologize for an error you or your company has made and, where needed, rectify the situation.

Whether you are making or responding to a complaint, sensitivity is paramount. Your communications must be professional and courteous even if you are frustrated and annoyed.

Depending on the nature of the problem, consider beginning with a phone call. It's more personal, more pleasant, and less formal. However, keep good records of when you call, to whom you speak, and what action, if any, is promised. If no action is taken, or the action is unsatisfactory, you may want to make a follow-up call or you may decide it's time to put the complaint in writing.

In business, complaints are usually made and responded to in a letter rather than an e-mail, but the status quo is evolving and e-mails are being used more and more frequently for this purpose. In general, it is safe to say that if you receive a complaint via e-mail, you may respond with an e-mail. If you receive a letter of complaint, you may respond by e-mail

- if the writer has asked that you do so
- if the writer has given you the option to do so
- if the complaint is so urgent that it requires an immediate response

In this last case, a telephone call might be the best approach. In some cases, a follow-up letter is valuable.

In most cases, if a complaint is about something very important, it is best to send a letter, which is more formal and provides a better record. You can even request a signature on delivery as proof of when and where it was delivered and who received it.

Normally, an internal issue between colleagues is not called a complaint; but, whatever you call it, you may need to tell someone in your own or another department that there is a problem. In such cases, a memo or an e-mail is appropriate.

> **SIMPLY STATED**
>
> No matter what form your complaint takes:
>
> - State the facts clearly and succinctly.
> - Provide all necessary information to get the complaint resolved (enclose copies of documents or correspondence, if necessary).
> - Say what action you want taken.
> - Suggest a reasonable timetable for action to be taken.
> - Be polite.
>
> Be sure to keep copies of letters, memos, or e-mails you write.

WHEN YOU HAVE A COMPLAINT

Sometimes you want to notify someone with whom you are dealing that you are dissatisfied with the service you've received. You are not asking for compensation or a replacement—in fact, you are not asking for any specific action—but you do want to let the recipient know that you are less than pleased. Such letters are important and can be helpful—and your correspondence should reflect that.

Complaint about Late Delivery

In the letter that follows, the writer begins with a compliment and then goes on to explain the problem.

> Dear Meredith,
>
> As you know, we are very pleased with the quality, design, and service we get from everyone at Joey and Jenny Swimwear. Our customers simply devour them and no matter how many we order, we can't seem to keep them in stock. They just keep flying off the racks.
>
> That's why we were so disappointed when for the second time a promised delivery date was missed. You and I spoke about this after the first late delivery. At the time, you were not sure whether the problem was in your warehouse or with the trucker you use. We'd be grateful if you would look into it again and let us know what can be done to avoid this problem in the future. We will be placing another order in about a month, and hope that you can resolve this problem before the next delivery.
>
> Many thanks for your help.
>
> Best Regards,

At other times, you are seeking action. When this is the case, you need to make certain that your letter conveys exactly what you expect; for example, replacement merchandise for an incorrect delivery, a refund, an adjustment, or similar.

Complaint about Incorrect Shipment

Dear Mr. Hank,

I'm writing to confirm our conversation this afternoon. As you know, we received a shipment of two dozen XYZ-137 widgets, when we, in fact, ordered three dozen GHQ-732 widgets. Enclosed is a copy of my original order, PZ-5370-06.

It would be appreciated if a pick-up of the XYZ-137 widgets and re-delivery of our original order of GHQ-732 widgets could be arranged, and my account properly credited for the incorrect shipment, including all shipping and handling charges.

Please call or e-mail to confirm these arrangements. Thank you for your attention.

Sincerely,

Follow-Up to a Complaint about an Incorrect Invoice

You should allow a reasonable amount of time before following up on a complaint. The amount of time that is reasonable depends on the situation. Some situations, such as an order missing in transit, require immediate attention; others, such as an incorrect invoice, may not need to be corrected until the next billing cycle.

To Customer Service Representative

Subject: Account #660730579, Invoice #10-3007642

Dear Marsha,

You may recall that our order #876-5 was duplicated and authorized to be returned to your company last month. Payment for the original single shipment, invoice #9-300183, was made two months ago; however, despite several conversations with Salvio Mendocino in accounts receivable, we are still receiving statements showing an outstanding balance.

You were so helpful in facilitating the return that I am hoping you may be able to help us here. As you know, we've been customers of

Bath Supplies Unlimited for years and have never experienced any problems.

I would appreciate anything you can do to expedite the credit. Thank you.

Sincerely,

To a Department Head

Subject: Account #660730579, Invoice #10-3007642

Dear Sid,

I wouldn't normally go to the head of the department about an invoice, but at this point, I have no other choice.

Six months ago, we received an order which was inadvertently duplicated by your shipping department. We immediately notified your customer service representative, Marsha, who sent us a return authorization (copy enclosed) and the supplies were promptly returned. Your invoice #9-300183 for our original single order was paid in full.

Despite repeated phone calls and e-mails, however, we have not received a credit for the duplicated shipment, and are now we are being hounded by your collection agency. You can imagine how frustrating this is. We have had a longstanding, productive relationship with you and Bath Supplies Unlimited, and don't want that to change. I'd be grateful if you could get this straightened out before the next billing cycle.

Many thanks.

Yours truly,

Enc.

Complaint about Poor or Inadequate Service

Dear Mr. Miller,

Your firm was contracted to paint our office at 40447 Alameda Street the week of July 23. According to our agreement, dated June 5, the work was to be completed within one week. Based on this assurance, we closed our office for the entire week and rented an office space near our facility.

As agreed, we were to inspect the premises on Friday afternoon at 2 P.M. Upon arrival, we found that work had not yet begun on three of the 12 rooms: two had received only a coat of primer, and one had only a single coat of paint applied. The remaining offices were complete although some areas required touching up and the entire office needed to be thoroughly cleaned as promised in your agreement. We pointed these discrepancies out to the foreman, Steve Patterson, and noted it on the punch list you provided at the start of the job (copy enclosed).

Subsequently, we have had to extend our short-term rental agreement for a second week at a cost of $3,200 (copy of lease agreement enclosed). Based on paragraph seven of your contract, this letter is our formal notification that we are invoking the penalty clause and will be deducting that amount from your invoice.

Sincerely,

Stanley S. Slocum, MD

Enc.

Complaint to a Coworker

It is generally best to try to resolve problems with your counterpart informally—in person or on the phone—and to keep higher-ups out of the loop. Occasionally, things have to be put in writing and someone else may be needed to help resolve the issue. The following is an example of a memo or e-mail you might send when other routes have failed.

Subject: Monthly Accounts Receivable Report

Ingrid,

As we've discussed several times by phone and in person, this report, which is due no later than the 10th of each month, has been arriving later and later. This month, we did not receive it until the 17th. Each day the report is delayed has a negative effect on our cash flow because it means that our collection staff can't get on the phone and follow up with our customers to expedite payment. It also means a delay in notifying the sales department to embargo deadbeats, which in the case of Jekyll Company cost us a bundle.

During our last conversation, I got the impression that the report was late because your department was understaffed, what with Kathy out on maternity leave and Joel in the hospital. As you can see, I've

copied this letter to Sam; perhaps he can authorize the hiring of some temporary help or lend you a person or two from the payables side to relieve the burden. I know you are doing the best you can under difficult circumstances, but I'm getting pressure from the controller's office, so we need to resolve this problem quickly.

If you have other ideas for how to get through this rough period, I'm eager for all suggestions.

Regards,

cc:

WHEN YOU ARE RESPONDING TO A COMPLAINT

Responses to complaints are a form of apology. When you or your firm makes an error, admit it, apologize for it, and correct it! In business, you may find yourself apologizing even when the person making the complaint is wrong. You may even find yourself "correcting" the error, although there are times when this is not possible, just to keep the customer or client happy.

SIMPLY STATED

When making an apology

- *admit mistake*
- *take responsibility for wrongdoing*
- *correct discrepancy, if possible*
- *if appropriate, suggest alternative or compromise*

Apologizing for a Defective Product

In the first example following, a store really doesn't know when or how the product got damaged, but nevertheless has accepted responsibility for it. In the second, the company does not believe it is responsible, but looks to satisfy the customer with a compromise. In the last example, the company denies the customer's request.

Dear Ms. DeSantos,

We were dismayed to learn that the glass bowl you purchased last week in Savannah had a small chip. Now that you are back in San Francisco, it would indeed be difficult for you to exchange it in person. May I suggest two alternatives? We can send a new bowl and authorize a pickup of the defective one—we would, of course, pay all shipping costs—or we can refund the amount to your credit card and arrange a pickup of the other.

Please let me know how you would like us to proceed, and we will take care of it immediately. We look forward to seeing you on your next visit to Savannah.

Sincerely yours,

Denying a Refund

Dear Mr. Gonzales,

We regret that the glass bowl you purchased six months ago has chipped. As you know, our glassware is fine hand-blown crystal and, therefore, very fragile. Although it is dishwasher safe, care must be taken that the piece does not touch other objects or move when the machine cycles. In the information sheet we provide with each purchase, hand washing and drying is recommended, and instructions for machine washing are also included.

Because you purchased the bowl six months ago, we cannot replace it free of charge. However, the bowl is in stock and I have enclosed a certificate for a 15% discount on the bowl or any other item in the shop. If it is more convenient to order by mail, I have enclosed our catalog so you can see some of our newer items as well.

We look forward to serving you again.

Very truly yours,

DID YOU KNOW?

You can learn a great deal about your company and products from letters of complaint; that's why some companies ask unhappy customers to let them know, and encourage their staff to view complaints seriously and with an open mind.

Dear Ms. Wang,

I have your letter regarding the glass bowl that you purchased in our Savannah store six weeks ago, and regret that you are dissatisfied with it. As I explained when you called last week, the bowl you purchased was sold "as is." The sign on the sale table noted that items on the table were slightly damaged and should be examined carefully prior to purchase since all sales were final.

Because the bowl had a slight imperfection, the price was 75% less than it would have been had it been perfect. You noted in your letter that the chip is in the rim. Many of our customers buy bowls such as yours for flower arrangements, which hide the chip entirely; others take the bowl to a glass repair shop where they can grind the imperfection out of the rim. I have enclosed a list of glass repairers in your area in the event you choose to go this route.

Sincerely,

Acknowledging a Problem

Remember the letter to Meredith at Joey and Jenny Swimwear (see page 51) about missed delivery dates? Here's how Meredith answered it.

> Dear Sally,
>
> Thank you so much for bringing the delivery issue to my attention again. I am sorry you had to tell me twice. The first time, I spoke with the warehouse manager, Jorge Santiago, who said it was a fluke and assured me it would not happen again. This time, I talked both to Jorge and to the chief of operations, Homer Bravado, and learned that we started using a new shipping company just around the time your problem began, and that yours was an early—but not the only—complaint.
>
> Homer has told the shipper that he will cancel the contract if he receives any more complaints and has asked me to tell you that there will be no shipping charges on your next two orders. When you place your next two orders, remember to give the person taking the order the following codes: CC08325-01 for the first order and CC08325-02 for the second.
>
> Thanks again for making me aware you were having a problem. We are delighted that you and your customers like the Joey and Jenny line of swimwear, and look forward to working with you in the future.
>
> Best regards,

CHAPTER SIX

Congratulations, Get Well Greetings, and Condolences

In Good Times and in Bad

Letters of congratulations and condolences are really personal letters, but the occasion can arise in the workplace for either kind of letter. Although you can buy a card with a preprinted message, a well-thought-out personal note—whether appended to a card or in a letter—is appreciated.

CONGRATULATIONS

The list of occasions on which you will send messages of congratulations is practically endless. A well-written congratulatory note will mean a great deal to the recipient; as an added benefit, it will demonstrate your thoughtfulness and strengthen your relationships with colleagues, clients, suppliers, and staff members.

Congratulatory notes can take any form, including handwritten notes, which are appropriate for any recipient and may make the biggest impression, especially if you use quality note cards or paper. In general, if you are congratulating someone outside your company, a letter or card will convey your message with the most impact; if you are writing to someone inside the firm, an e-mail is appropriate. (For someone you see often or are particularly close with, a call or face-to-face congratulation is always welcome.)

Congratulation letters that you write for business are very similar to those you might send a friend or relative and cover more personal topics such as

- a promotion or a new job
- closing a big deal or sale
- retirement

In some cases, it is appropriate to congratulate a business associate or colleague on

- the birth or adoption of a child
- engagement or marriage

Just how personal your note is will depend on your relationship to the individual.

To a Colleague on a Promotion

Subject: Your Promotion

Jake,

I just heard the news! You'll make a terrific production manager; no one deserves it more than you. I'm really looking forward to working with you in your new role; and, please call if I can be of any assistance during the transition.

Best of luck,

To a Customer on a Promotion

Dear Sarah,

I just got the announcement. Congratulations. You are going to be a great VP for marketing; you really deserve it. My only regret is that when you assume your new position, we won't be working as closely together as we do now.

I'd love to take you for a celebratory lunch at Guido's next week. I'll call to see what day works for you.

With all best wishes for your continued success,

Jackie

For a Job Well Done

Subject: Sunshine Shoe Order

Chris,

What can I say? We had been trying to crack Sunshine for years before you arrived. Once you got here, the orders started coming our way slowly but surely. This latest order is bigger than any we've had, not only from Sunshine but from any customer of similar size. Whatever magic you are working—and I know how hard you have been working—keep up the good work.

By the way, when you get back to the office next week, we'd like to have a small celebration at Dominick's Steak Joint. Does Thursday work for you?

See you when you get back.

Subject: Excellent Job!

Norm,

I just got the third quarter results. You and your team exceeded your goals by more than 25%. This was particularly impressive because I know the group was operating under pressure, what with the move to new facilities.

I will be announcing this achievement in the company newsletter, which will be posted on the intranet next week, but I wanted members of Production Team Two to know immediately how gratified the Board and I are at their accomplishment.

Keep up the excellent work!

On a Boss's Retirement

When writing any retirement letter, it's a good idea to begin with something personal about working with the person and, of course, to mention something about the person's accomplishments. If your relationship allows, say something personal about what the retiree will be doing. Whatever you say, it's important to keep the focus on the person, not on you.

Dear Jim,

We have worked together for ten years now, and have experienced many adventures together as you built this division from a 10-person shop to a team of 150. It is hard to believe that in a few more days I won't hear your booming voice as you come down the hall rousing spirits in hard times (and there were a few) and urging us to bigger and better heights in good times (there were many).

I know you are looking forward to writing your book and fly-fishing in Montana: No one deserves it more than you do. As you no doubt know, you will be missed—not only by me and the team, but by all those who have worked with you inside the company and out.

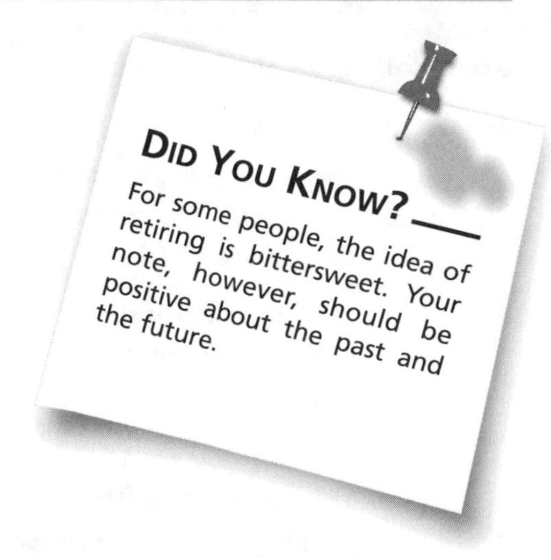

When writing to a business colleague or acquaintance you don't know well, don't get too gushy or personal, and don't presume too much. Unless you really know "how much they wanted a baby," or "what they went through adopting a child," or "how much you love Tom," don't say it.

To a Coworker on the Birth of a Child

Dear Steve,

Stan just announced that you and Amy had a boy, and that mother and son are doing well. At 9 lbs. 12 oz., it looks like he's going to take after you, and will be playing varsity tackle with an eye toward the NFL!

See you when you get back from paternity leave; in the meantime, congratulations and best wishes,

To a Customer on Marriage

Dear Ruth,

I just wanted you to know how happy I am for you. While I don't know Tom, he must be a wonderful man for you to have chosen him. I wish both of you great happiness on Sunday and throughout the years to come.

With warmest good wishes,

GET WELL GREETINGS

No matter what the nature of the illness, your letter should express concern and sympathy, and its tone should be upbeat; however, if the illness is serious, it should not convey false optimism. If you offer help, be prepared to give it if asked.

To a Colleague after an Accident

Dear Noah,

I had lunch with Jessica the other day. She said you had broken your ankle in a skiing accident over the holiday. What a way to begin the new year!

I know you were looking forward to the annual buyers' convention, but Jess said that although you were mending well, you had to stay off it for a few more weeks, so you won't be there. We are going to miss you.

I'll be back in town for the mid-year meetings; let's plan on getting together for drinks and dinner.

Best wishes,

To an Office Friend in the Hospital

Dear Marcy,

We all hope you are feeling better after the surgery on Tuesday. Sarah said your mom called to say you were doing well, and that you were beginning to feel stronger and would be home by Saturday. When you are strong enough for company, I would like to come by the house one day after work. I'll call next week to see how you are doing.

Everyone in the department wants you to know that they miss you. I especially miss our lunchtime chats.

Wishing you a speedy and full recovery,

CONDOLENCES

When you send a sympathy letter to a business acquaintance, whether the person works for your company or for another, your message should convey sincere feeling. Because it is likely you do not know the person who died, it would sound false to write about that person except in the most general terms. Instead, the focus of your thoughts and the letter should be on how your colleague must feel.

The one exception would be when writing to the family of a colleague or business acquaintance who has died.

On the Death of a Spouse

Here the writer makes an offer of support. Such offers should not be made unless you are prepared to give the aid offered.

Dear Brian:

I was saddened to hear of Maureen's death. Although I only met her once, her warmth, intelligence, and vivacity were immediately apparent. Please extend my sympathies to your children and the rest of your family. If you need a shoulder to lean on when you return to the office, please know that I am here for you.

Sincerely,

On the Death of a Family Member

If you are the human resources liaison or head of a department or the company, you may be writing on behalf of the staff.

Dear Sally,

I would like to extend our deepest sympathy to you and your family on the death of your mother.

Louise was a vital member of our team. Her warm laugh, coupled with her dedication, creativity, and indomitable spirit, are among the many memories we shall keep of her. We will miss her.

Sincerely,

CHAPTER **SEVEN**

Credit and Collection

Worth the Effort

Most businesses, perhaps even more than individuals, rely on credit. New businesses in particular—especially small ones—must apply for credit from banks and other lenders, suppliers, technicians, service firms, and others. Loans provide part of the operating capital businesses require as they grow; this capital allows them to purchase the materials and supplies they need to create their product, to pay staff salaries and benefits, and so on.

Except for bank loans, where printed applications are the rule, most businesses apply for credit by letter. If the business is small or new, it probably has not established a credit rating with any of the rating companies, so the supplier relies on information from banks and others who have done business with the company. Because of the need for confidentiality and a formal record, a letter is typically used for the initial request for credit, the creditors' request for information from a reference, and the response they receive.

Of course, credit is not only for small or new business. Long-established businesses with plenty of money to pay their bills need credit just to facilitate purchases, which is why most businesses operate on credit. Consider how awkward it would be if you had to have someone with cash or a check at the warehouse every time a shipment was received! Besides, even profitable businesses have the occasional cash flow problem. Many customers owe them money; the customers are going to pay their bills; but the money is not in hand at the moment the business needs to purchase additional supplies. At such times, credit is a useful tool.

APPLICATION FOR CREDIT

Sometimes a person—especially a young person—starting a small business will provide personal as well as professional references to establish creditworthiness.

Initial Request for Credit

Dear Mr. Berman,

Enclosed is the itemized PO #3732-101 for assorted vegetables. Our restaurant will open on April 1, and we anticipate placing similar orders weekly. We would like to open an account on your normal terms, but, as you suggested when we spoke, I have enclosed check #1236 for $232.50 to expedite the initial purchase.

You may check our credit with:

Restaurant Supply Co., 15 Vanderbilt Avenue, Chicago, IL 60660
Fine Linens, Inc., 103-46 East 17th Street, Long Island City, NY 10537
Bank of America, 206 Easton Avenue, Somerset, NJ 08873

Should you wish to check my personal credit, you may do so at the same Bank of America branch, where I have a personal line of credit and an auto loan.

If you need additional information, please let me know. We look forward to receiving the first order and word on your credit decision as soon as possible.

Sincerely,

Request for Credit Information from a Reference

Dear Ms. Smythe:

Richard Marks of Food and Film has applied for credit with us and listed Fine Linens, Inc. as a credit reference.

We would appreciate any information you can provide about Food and Film's credit rating. How long have you known Mr. Marks and how long he has had an account with you? How many orders has he placed on credit? Were his payments made in a timely fashion or have any of his debts been overdue? Your response will, of course, be held in the strictest confidence.

Enclosed is a SASE for your convenience.

Sincerely,

Enc.

Responding to a Request for a Credit Reference

The first example for response is positive; the second not. In either case, when you respond, stick to the facts: how much, how long, how often, and so on. Doing more than that could embroil you in legal issues of libel or misrepresentation.

Dear Mr. Berman:

Here is the confidential information you requested about Richard Marks and Food and Film.

Mr. Marks placed his first order with us for $750 worth of kitchen equipment in February of this year. Since that time, he has ordered several major appliances: an oven and salamander on June 3, for $5,000; two stainless sinks on June 17 for $3,750; and two industrial refrigerator/freezers on July 3 for $20,000. Our terms initially (the first two orders) were net 15 days. After prompt payment and at Mr. Marks's request, we extended him our normal discount of net 30 days. He continued to make prompt payment.

Prior to starting this new venture, Mr. Marks was the head chef at Catch as Catch Can for five years, and in that capacity, made many purchases from our firm. Based on this relationship, we extended him a higher level of initial credit than we might otherwise have done.

Sincerely,

Dear Mr. Berman:

Richard Marks of Food and Film opened an account with us on January 23, and placed his first order on January 30, amounting to $395. He continued placing orders of about the same size each month through August. Until then, all invoices were paid on time under our terms of net 30 days. The July order was paid in 45 days; however, the August and September orders, which were the last we accepted, have still not been paid.

As you indicated in your letter, we would appreciate it if you kept this information confidential.

Sincerely,

Granting a Request for Credit

Dear Mr. Marks,

We hope you were pleased with your first order from Farm Fresh Fruits and Veggies, and it is our pleasure to welcome you into our family of credit customers. For the first six months, we will extend a maximum monthly credit of $1,000, after which time we can reevaluate your needs and credit history to extend that limit.

As we discussed, our terms are net 30 days. Your account representative, Susan Shelley, can answer any questions you may have and will keep you posted on specials, new products, and availability and quality of seasonal merchandise. She will call to introduce herself and familiarize you with our many services.

Thank you for choosing Farm Fresh Fruits and Veggies, and good luck in your new venture.

Sincerely,

Refusing a Request for Credit

This letter is tricky. You don't want to offend the potential customer—his business might succeed—therefore, you would like him to purchase from you on a cash basis until such time as his credit rating improves and you feel comfortable extending credit. It is also important that you maintain the confidentiality of the information his references supplied.

Throughout this book, we have advised that you be direct and to the point; here, less is definitely more.

Dear Mr. Marks:

We hope you were pleased with your first order from Farm Fresh Fruits and Veggies. We appreciate your recent request for credit. However, our independent credit agency's report indicates that your business does not have sufficient credit history for us to extend credit to Food and Film at this time.

We hope you will continue to order your produce from us on a COD basis; in all other ways, you will receive the same personalized service our credit customers receive. After Food and Film has become more established, you can reapply, and we will be happy to reevaluate your request.

As you know, Farm Fresh Fruits and Veggies offers the highest quality produce for the best price in the region, and we look forward to serving you again.

Sincerely,

SIMPLY STATED

The tone of collection letters will vary depending on whether you are trying to collect from another business or from an individual consumer. However, they all boil down to

- how much
- how long
- what to do
- by what date

DID YOU KNOW?

Whether you are a freelancer, an independent contractor, or a small business that knows its clients personally, it's often best to start the collection process with a friendly phone call. This often does the trick.

REQUESTS FOR LATE PAYMENT

For businesses, there are two types of collection letters; those that go to individual consumers and those that go from one business to another. The words and tone may vary a bit, but the gist is virtually the same.

E-Mail from a Freelancer to a Client

Subject: Help!

Susie,

It was great talking with you last week about the new project, and I'm looking forward to getting started on it. As I mentioned at the end of our conversation, I still have not received payment on the logo I designed for the launch of the new game. I know you approved the invoice, but it's now more than 30 days old, and I'd appreciate your looking into what's holding it up. Perhaps it's stuck somewhere on someone's desk. I'd be so grateful if you could pry it loose. I've attached a copy, just in case it fell behind someone's filing cabinet.

Many thanks for your help.

Best,

Series of Collection Letters

Some firms, such as catalogers and mail order sellers, hire professionals to write effective collection letters. The nature of their business means credit checking is sometimes cursory, and therefore, collecting money is more difficult. For most businesses, collection letters follow a pattern similar to the one that follows.

Collecting money actually begins with the invoice, which is enclosed with the shipment or mailed to the client. Most companies automatically send monthly statements, that indicate whether any money is past due and how long—usually 30, 60, or 90 days. Sometimes companies follow up with a second statement stamped *PAST DUE* to get your attention.

Collection letters require finesse—a combination of tact, diplomacy, and firmness. Especially when sent to individuals, their tone should be persuasive rather than punitive; only as they progress does the tone become increasingly stern. After all, in most cases, you still want to keep the customer. For some companies, three is the magic number, for others it may be five, for some even more; but eventually, if payment isn't made, the account is usually turned over to a collection agency or a law firm.

Did You Know?

If you rarely send collection letters and you have a personal relationship with the customer, address him or her personally; for larger companies, if your computer program allows you to personalize the salutation, it's a good idea to do so. If not, *Dear Customer*, or a variation of that, is used by many businesses.

Collection letters are usually signed with a name and title—often, Credit Manager. In some companies, the final letter is signed by a higher-up; for example, Controller or Business Manager.

First Collection Letter

There is some difference of opinion among professionals about the phrasing of the first letter. Some recommend a formal, impersonal note—just a statement of facts; others recommend going straight to the persuasive strategy. We give a sample of each: first the formal, then the persuasive.

> Dear Customer,
>
> Our records show a balance of $723.45 that is now 45 days past due. Payment in full by return mail is requested.
>
> Sincerely,

> Dear Customer,
>
> Did you know that your account was past due? We know that sometimes in the everyday rush, bills get buried. If you have not already sent in your payment for $723.45, please do so now. If you have, thank you for your payment, and please disregard this statement.

Second Collection Letter

Sometimes the second letter takes the tack of suggesting that there is a problem with the service or merchandise, or it may refer to the person's history excellent history with the company (or both). It may also suggest the possibility that you may not be able to fulfill future orders or that the customer will miss out on special offers. This technique can work especially well if you are dunning a business.

> Dear Customer,
>
> Have we done something wrong? Was there a problem with the product you purchased (or service we provided)? If so, please call the number on our letterhead to discuss the matter.
>
> You are a valued customer, and we would not like to see you miss out on the many special offers coming up this holiday season. Your current balance of $723.45 is 45 days past due; please send a check immediately.
>
> Sincerely,

Third Collection Letter

This letter is still friendly, but at the same time, it reminds customers that they may be jeopardizing their credit rating.

> Dear Customer,
>
> We cannot understand why, after 60 days, your balance of $723.45 remains unpaid. You are a valued customer, and we would not like to see you jeopardize your credit standing. To continue receiving credit on future purchases, please send a check today so that we may continue to extend this convenient service.

Fourth Collection Letter

In this letter, you may want to suggest that the customer may be having financial difficulties, and suggest he or she contact you. If the customer responds, you may be able to work out a payment plan.

> Dear Customer:
>
> Your account is long past due, and your credit rating is in serious jeopardy. The outstanding balance of $723.45 is now 75 days overdue. To protect your good credit standing, please pay this amount immediately.
>
> If you are having financial difficulties, call me at the above number, so we may discuss your options.
>
> We look forward to receiving payment or hearing from you immediately.
>
> Sincerely,

Fifth Collection Letter

If you still have not been paid, you may have no other choice but to turn the account over to a collection agency, or—if the amount is large—you may choose to take legal action instead.

Dear Customer,

FINAL NOTICE

Your account is 120 days past due. Despite many letters, you have neither settled your account nor called our office, as we suggested, to arrange for alternative ways to settle the matter.

Therefore, if we do not receive payment in full—$723.45—in five days, we will have no other choice but to turn your account over to a collection agency to recover this amount.

Sincerely,

CHAPTER **EIGHT**

Customer Correspondence

Spreading the Word

You have just passed two major customer correspondence hurdles—complaints and credit and collection letters—probably among the most difficult, although routine, customer correspondence you'll ever have to write.

Customer correspondence is a broad term covering the gamut of all other writing that flows between companies and their customers, including announcements (see Chapter 4) and replies to inquiries (see Chapter 12).

This chapter focuses on letters that sell—from everyday communication that goes regularly between businesses and their customers to more formal, less routine sales letters that must be customized to fit a very specific situation or proposal. In the first category, the emphasis is on informative communications and on keeping-in-touch or goodwill notes that are the bread and butter of all businesses. The second category includes the letters that accompany formal proposals and sales presentations to clients and customers.

DAY-TO-DAY CONTACTS WITH CUSTOMERS

For some sales letters, e-mail is the fastest and least expensive way to keep in touch with customers, although, as with anything e-mailed, there is always the danger of your e-mail getting lost in a crowded inbox. Here, a carefully worded subject line can make the difference between your message being opened, overlooked, or immediately dumped in the trash. The last two can easily happen if, rushing through the folder, the customer does not immediately recognize your name.

Since you are rarely communicating something critical, the reason for most of this correspondence is to keep you, your products, and your company in the customer's mind and to maintain a positive image. Telephone calls, face-to-face meetings or business lunches or dinners, and frequent (but not too frequent) written messages help keep a new customer happy and an old customer from drifting away or being enticed by the new guy on the block. Everyone wants to feel wanted—even in business.

As with all communications, what you say and how you say it counts, but when your reason for writing is to enhance your image, it counts more than ever.

> **SIMPLY STATED**
>
> - Target your message—for example, don't send the accounts payable manager information about technical matters.
> - Be friendly, but professional.
> - Don't overcommunicate—be brief and to the point.
> - Don't flood your customer's inbox.
> - Be selective about your message:
>   - ☐ Does your customer *need* this information?
>   - ☐ Will your customer *want* this information?
>   - ☐ Don't sell, at least not directly—these are *not* sales letters.

Informative Communications

The following e-mail is actually a subtle form of selling under the guise of letting the customer know that, because of the new tax law, the price of work he is considering will go up.

Subject: New tax on landscaping

Dear Simcha,

Did you know that beginning on January 1, a new state law goes into effect that requires landscapers to charge tax on all the work they do? That means the state no longer considers landscaping a capital improvement. The good news is that the law does not affect patios and decks.

It was great seeing you at the fair last week. Please say hello to Sarah.

Best regards,

Invitations

Subject: "Come Raise a Glass in a Pre-New Year Toast!"

Back, by popular demand, we are holding our pre-holiday "bubbly" seminar.

This year, we'll introduce you to our latest discoveries. While we can't call them champagne, as they are not all from that illustrious

French locale, there will be samplings from some of the most renowned French labels. In addition, we will be introducing fine sparkling wines from around the world, including the United States, as well as many other countries you may not have known had mastered the fine art of making outstanding sparkling wines.

Our guest speakers will be Jean Louis Fournier, author of numerous books; the vintner Mark Ghiardelli; and the famed restaurateur, Sharon Mellon, who has agreed to prepare the accompaniments for our tasting.

We hope you can join us. Because seating is limited, please RSVP to Sylvia Schneid, 732-469-1438.

Thank-You Notes

Thank-you notes are particularly nice when they come in the mail on little note cards, and even nicer when they are handwritten. Depending on your business, you may not always have time for this little touch, but a thank-you note, letter, or e-mail is always appreciated.

Dear Mrs. Coleman,

Thank you for choosing Fashion Fabrics for your window treatments. We hope you are enjoying them in your dining room as much as you did when you were in the shop. It was a pleasure serving you.

Yours sincerely,

Customer Referrals

Referrals, both when you make them and when you get them, are a good way to keep in touch. Even asking for them can be effective. The thank-you note above gives you a perfect opportunity to ask for a referral with the addition of one line.

P.S. Don't forget about our referral policy. Tell your friends to mention your name when they order any item in the shop, and you will receive a 5% discount on your next purchase.

E-mail is your best bet for the referral and thank you that follow.

DID YOU KNOW?

A P.S. can be the most effective part of your letter. Direct mail marketers use them all the time to call attention to an important piece of information that might be overlooked in the body of the letter.

Subject: May I pass your name along?

Hi, Sam,

I had dinner the other night with Travis Schuyler, a business client from a law firm in your area with whom we're doing business. He mentioned he was in the market for a new home and hadn't been happy with his previous agent. I think you'd be a good match. He's a great guy, and I think he's serious—not just a looker. May I give him your name and number?

It would be great to get together. The next time I'm in your neck of the woods, I'll let you know.

Regards,

Whether you accept a referral or turn it down, always acknowledge it and thank the person for it.

Subject: Thank you!

Cyril,

How nice of you to think of me. Yes, please give Travis my "vital statistics."

And yes, dinner would be lovely. It's beautiful here right now, so if you want to take a drive up the Taconic, you'll be in for a fall treat. Hope to see you soon.

FORMAL CUSTOMER CONTACTS

Often more formal sales letters are needed, for example, a cover letter for a proposal to a client or a response to a potential buyer. Some sales letters—direct mail letters, for instance—are actually a form of advertising and require special talents, skills, and training, and are beyond the scope of this chapter. Others may be written by various people in a company—the sales representative or manager, the owner of a small business, or someone in new product development: It depends mostly on the size of the company and the nature of the product.

Response to a Prospect

A prospect is a potential or prospective customer. In this case, the writer is trying to qualify the prospect—to find out whether the customer is serious about purchasing the product or is just looking, has the money to pay for the product, and is the decisionmaker. Follow the customer's lead in deciding whether to respond by mail or e-mail.

If you need to enclose brochures or catalogs, mail may be your only choice unless you have the material in electronic form, in which case you can attach it or refer the person to your website.

Dear Ms. Kenyon,

Thank you for your recent letter expressing an interest in purchasing one of our Tri-Star Kitchen Appliance franchises. I've enclosed a packet of information that covers our basic requirements for a franchisee and provides an overview of the services we provide in return.

However, for me to help you really understand the power that Tri-Star provides, I need to know more about you and your organization; for example, are you seeking a franchise for Topeka or for other locations as well? What size operation are you contemplating? What is your experience in the industry?

Please call me directly at the number above so that we can begin a discussion that will lead you to becoming one of our leading franchisees.

Sincerely,

Cover Letters

Dear Jacqueline,

Following up on our conversation Tuesday, I have prepared a packet of material that I believe will interest you. It contains—among other things—statistics on recent home building and renovations in Topeka, which as you will see is at an all-time high, as well as information about the average cost of new kitchens, which appliances have proven to be the most popular over the past three years, and demographic trends for the region. By the way, this is an example of the kind of support we regularly provide our dealerships.

I think this information will assist you as you formulate the business plan we will need when we consider your application for a franchise.

Don't hesitate to call if you have any questions about Tri-Star or your plan. We are here to help you create a successful enterprise.

Best regards,

Follow-Up to a Meeting or a Presentation

Dear Chris,

It was great meeting with you and your European counterparts on Monday. The project is unique and continues to intrigue us because of the challenges and opportunities it presents. We are eager to join you and your colleagues in bringing it to life.

We can work together in several ways:

1. Our agency would represent you in the United States, and would receive a 15% commission on any monies received in connection with any editions or versions of the game(s) as well as any subsidiary or ancillary rights sold.
2. Our agency can package (or produce) the game(s). Here our role can include artistic and aesthetic decisions or be limited to just the technical aspects of producing the prototype or manufacturing the final product. (Flat fee to be based upon the nature of our involvement or expenses, plus advance against royalty to be negotiated.)
3. Our agency can provide consulting on all aspects of the project. (Fees to be determined on project or hourly basis.)

Regardless of the route(s) taken, the initial steps as outlined at the meeting are identical and should be completed and approved no later than June 15. At that time, too, you and your group will have determined what role you want Jenkins Associates to play, and we will have an agreement in place so that we will be able to move on to the next phase in July.

Let me know if you have any questions; if we don't speak sooner, I look forward to our meeting next week.

Best,

CHAPTER **NINE**

The Job Search

When the Product Is You

We all look for jobs at some point in our careers. There was a time when people found a job and stuck with it, sometimes for an entire career. For a variety of reasons, that's become less and less common. Whether by choice or of necessity, you will probably find yourself looking for something else, somewhere else. Many people enjoy the hunt, others dislike it, but whether you love it or hate it or fall somewhere in between, it's an inevitable part of working life.

Writing is a critical part of the search for a new position. Of course, you will need to prepare a resume, but in addition, you may also need to write

- networking letters or e-mails
- requests for information
- information interview requests
- cover letters or e-mails
- thank-you letters
    - o for the interview
    - o for the job offer

And, once you land that job, you'll probably be writing a

- letter of resignation

Letters you write when you are looking for a job are like sales letters, but in this case the product you are selling is *you*. For this reason, the letters you write have to be as perfect as you can make them. That means that you must think not only about what you say and how you say it, but also about grammar, spelling, and even the paper your letter is written on.

NETWORKING

Networking is often the best route to a good job. You never know who in your network will provide a lead, so it is best to contact everyone you know, including friends, relatives, acquaintances, colleagues, business associates, club or church members, and so on in order to spread the word that you are in the market for a new position and to find out what is out there.

To network with friends and relatives, you may prefer to call them, or talk to them at regular get-togethers. With others, you may wish to send either a letter or an e-mail, depending on your relationship with them. Unless told otherwise, it's safe to assume that you can send an e-mail to a friend or colleague, but you should send a letter to someone you don't know, or know only casually.

DID YOU KNOW?

If you are looking for a job before you have left the old one, your search needs to be discreet and less scattershot than it would be if you were unemployed. For example, answering a blind ad—one that doesn't name the company—could be risky, as you could be applying to the company you want to leave. Also, people in an industry often know one another; make certain those you contact are aware of your situation, so that they don't inadvertently let the cat out of the bag.

To a Business Acquaintance

Dear John,

As by now I think you know, the textile fiber division of Deuce Chemical has been sold and is moving to Tuscaloosa. I was unable to say anything sooner because of SEC regulations. I've been asked to stay on as part of the transition team, and will be here for another six months. If you need anything, I'll be here to handle things until August 15.

My plans for the future are open, although I would like to stay in the Roanoke area if possible. If you hear of anything you think would be up my alley, I'd be grateful for a heads up.

Best regards,

As always when you are looking for a job, as soon as you get a lead from someone in your network, you should strike while the iron is hot and immediately write to that person. Depending on the type of lead, the letter is similar to those you send in response to ads or to companies or individuals without a specific job opening, but with whom you would like to work. However, the fact that you have been recommended can make the letter a little easier to write, and may make the reader more responsive to your request.

Follow-Up to a Networking Lead

Dear Ms. Griffith,

Andy Hardy at Precision Drafting Tools mentioned that Miniature Models is looking for a sales manager for the Southwest.

I currently represent Tiny Tintypes in New Mexico, Arizona, and Colorado, with whom I've worked for the past three years. I have been in the industry for the past ten years, and am very familiar with—and have long admired—the Miniature Models line. The fine craftsmanship is visible in every piece you make. It would be a great pleasure to be associated with your company and to help it expand its sales in the Southwest.

I have enclosed my resume, and would appreciate the opportunity to meet with you to explore ways in which this could be accomplished.

Sincerely,

REQUEST FOR INFORMATION

In the following example, the jobseeker has used a networking lead to request information, but a similar letter could be written cold to someone whose name you may have obtained on a website or from an article you read or a story you heard on the news.

Dear Ms. Williams,

Regina Rosario gave me your name as someone who could provide information on the electronics industry.

I recently graduated from Stevens Institute, where I majored in electrical engineering. I am eager to find a position in the electronics industry. Regina thought you were the ideal person to advise me on career opportunities, both in the New York metropolitan area and in the Midwest, which is where my family lives.

I'd greatly appreciate any thoughts and advice you would be willing to share.

Very truly yours,

REQUEST FOR AN INFORMATION INTERVIEW

A request for an information interview is similar to an information request. It, too, is a form a networking. Most often, though, you will be writing cold. Unlike in the request above, here you have chosen this person because the industry or the company is one you have targeted. However, instead of asking for a job, you take the indirect approach of asking for information about the industry or the company. Such letters are long shots but, with the right letter, the door just might open. Then, it's up to how well you come across in the interview. Even if there's no job at the time, there may be one in the future, or your inquiry might lead to a positive lead, which, after all, is what this is all about.

> Dear Mr. Kingsolver,
>
> I read the recent *Forbes* article on Kingsolver, Wright & Riley with much enthusiasm. I have been keenly interested in architectural design ever since I saw Mies van der Rohe's sketches at MoMA when I was ten, and I have studied and admired your designs over the years since. I did my undergraduate work at the Pratt Institute in New York, and, in June, I will receive my Master's in Architecture from the University of California, Berkeley.
>
> As you can imagine, I have many questions about the industry, and many decisions to make about what my next steps should be. For example, should I go abroad and study classical architecture or Far Eastern forms, as some of my professors have urged? Would it be best to join a small firm, where I might get opportunities to work on my own projects faster, or would I learn more by joining a large firm and apprenticing with the masters?
>
> I am certain you are very busy, but might it be possible to fit me in for 30 minutes to explore some of these questions? I know I would gain a great deal from your knowledge and experience. I will call on Tuesday to set up a meeting, if you are amenable.
>
> Thank you in advance for your consideration.
>
> Sincerely,

THANK-YOU NOTE FOR INFORMATION OR FOR AN INFORMATION INTERVIEW

Don't forget to thank everyone who gave you a lead or provided information. As your job search continues, you may want to keep your contacts posted periodically and, when you locate a position, let them know. People like to feel that their contribution is appreciated, especially if it bore fruit.

Dear Mr. Wigon,

Thank you so much for meeting with me yesterday. I learned a lot about the state of Wall Street today and what it takes to succeed as a financial planner. Thank you, too, for introducing me to Cynthia Lane. Her comments about pursuing a CFP and going to graduate school made me rethink my plans about jumping right in after I graduate. Although I haven't made a final decision, I am seriously contemplating graduate school, and have begun exploring work-study opportunities. I cannot impose on my parents to support me for several more years.

I will of course let you know what I decide, and keep you posted on my progress. Thank you again for your invaluable input.

Sincerely,

DID YOU KNOW?

When sending your resume by e-mail, unless instructed to include it in the body of the e-mail, attach it as a Word, WordPerfect, or RTF (rich text format) document. It will be more attractive and easier to read because it will retain its formatting. If your system allows you to paste your resume into an e-mail, paste it as a text-only or plain-text version; if your system doesn't have this capability, format it using your word-processing program and then paste it into your e-mail.

COVER LETTERS OR E-MAILS

Cover letters (more and more today, they are e-mails) are crucial to a successful job search. More than the resume, which is more or less a statement of facts, the cover letter is where you must sell yourself and distinguish yourself from all other applicants. It's where you blow your own horn, but without seeming to brag.

A cover letter gives you an opportunity to say something positive about yourself, and to tailor your qualifications to the specific job and the company. You can do this by referring to something in your resume and expanding on it to demonstrate why your qualifications make you the perfect choice for the job. On the other hand, if your background is not exactly what the company has outlined in their ad, you can use your cover letter to turn what might seem to be a negative into a positive. In either case, you need to stress the contribution you could make to the company.

You may write a cover letter in response to a networking lead or an advertisement, or you may write it cold. In the last category, you might target specific companies for which you would like to work, or target all companies in a particular industry and/or in a particular area, such as all nursery schools within 20 miles of your home.

SIMPLY STATED

Cover letters should be

- well written
- error free
- positive and enthusiastic

They should demonstrate your

- knowledge
- interest in the company
- interest in the position

To a Networking Lead

This letter can be more friendly and personal than a letter responding to an ad or a cold letter. At the same time, the writer must express enthusiasm for the job and the company. In the following letter, the writer uses the opportunity to explain why she is leaving her present employer.

Dear Deborah,

Thanks so much for calling. When Steve gave me your name, I did not expect that there might be an opening at the bank.

Chicago Trust is a true leader in the banking industry, and I knew that they were expanding into full-service brokerage, but thought that was only being done out of New York. I am delighted to learn that CT is offering those services right here in Chicago.

As Steve may have mentioned, I have been working in the trading department of BGG Securities for the past five years, and have now completed my Series 7 exam and have become a fully licensed broker. BGG, the company with whom I am affiliated, is closing its Chicago office and consolidating its brokerage activities in New York. My husband is a professor at the Chicago School of Economics, a job he loves, so it's really not possible for me to make the move.

As you suggested, I have enclosed my resume. Your offer to pass it along personally to Tom Balaban and to put in a good word for me is really above and beyond what I had expected; thank you so much. I'll let you know what happens.

Sincerely,

In Response to an Ad

If the name of the company is not mentioned, you cannot address why you would like to work for the particular company, but you can stress your experience and interest in the field.

> Dear Mr. Hwang,
>
> I saw your ad in the Sunday, June 6 edition of the *New York Times* for a senior claims administrator for a major healthcare provider.
>
> As the enclosed resume demonstrates, I have been in the industry for the past ten years; most recently with National Health, Inc., where I have been a claims administrator for the past three years. Previously, I worked for St. Simeon's Hospital, first as an insurance claims assistant and then as claims manager. Working on both sides of the industry has given me a broad understanding of the problems that can arise, and insights into how to expedite and settle them to the satisfaction of all concerned—including the patient.
>
> I look forward to meeting you in person to discuss my qualifications. I can be reached in the evenings, after 6 P.M., at 616-777-6666, or during the day on my cell phone, 793-243-0673.
>
> Sincerely,

Follow-Up to Letter Sent in Response to an Ad

> Dear Mr. Hwang,
>
> Two weeks ago, I sent my resume in response to your ad in the *New York Times* for a senior claims administrator. I am very interested in the position and believe my work experience as a claims administrator for the past three years at National Health and as a claims assistant and then manager at St. Simeon's Hospital would be an asset to your firm.
>
> Please let me know if I can provide further information. I look forward to hearing from you regarding an interview.
>
> Sincerely,

To a Targeted Company

This approach is not for the timid, because you have to put yourself out there. Some companies and industries are more amenable to this approach than others are. It takes a great deal of work and a lot of fortitude. For it to succeed, you really have to do your homework. Find newspaper stories and magazine articles, and visit the company's website. Get to know the company inside out. The more you know, the more impressive your letter will be, and the easier it will be to demonstrate how your strengths will contribute to the company.

To paraphrase John F. Kennedy, ask not what the company can do for you, tell the company what you can do for it.

Dear Mr. Bruno,

I have been following the fortunes of the Bruno & Battaglia Vineyards ever since I joined the Flint Valley Wineries seven years ago as a sales representative for the Eastern Division. At the time, you were the new kid on the block, producing a few wines, all of which were of the highest quality. Over the years, you have expanded the types of wines you offered, but clearly all were carefully tested and, again, all have been of top-of-the-line quality. When I learned last week that you had acquired G & G Vineyards in the Willamette Valley, another excellent producer, it solidified my desire to join forces with you.

The only area in which Bruno & Battaglia Vineyards has not made the inroads I would have anticipated is in market penetration. As the enclosed resume shows, I am now Flint Valley Wineries' national sales manager, and am deeply involved not only with managing our 100 sales representatives nationwide, but with the advertising and marketing of the various brands as well. When I took on that position three years ago, like B&B today, we had only 25 representatives, and sales were one-tenth of what they are today. Knowing the quality of your product, as I do, I am convinced I could contribute to similar growth at B&B.

I hope you will agree to meet with me when I am in San Francisco in two weeks, or at some other convenient time. I will call your office next week or you can reach me at the number or e-mail address above. Thank you for your consideration.

Sincerely,

To a Broad List of Companies

It's harder, but worth the effort, to customize your letter and find out the name of the person to whom you would report—for example, the director of marketing. If for some reason you can't find out that person's name, the next best thing is to find out the name of the human resources manager and address her or him by name.

> Dear Mr. Feldman,
>
> I recently graduated from the City College of Kansas City with a BS degree in chemistry, and am seeking an entry-level position in biochemical engineering. The two summers I spent interning at Buddenbrooks Corporation convinced me that I wanted to specialize in this area.
>
> Along with my resume, I have enclosed letters of recommendation from Dr. Eugene Stanton, Dean of the Chemistry Department at the college, and Sarah Siddons, director of the lab in which I worked at Buddenbrooks.
>
> Your company's position as an industry leader, its dynamic research program, and its outstanding reputation led me to write to you. I am willing, eager to learn (I plan to attend night school and gradually earn my doctorate), and enjoy challenges. I know I would learn a great deal, and believe that over time I could contribute to Clarion's history of success.
>
> I hope you will meet with me to discuss what opportunities are available at Clarion for an energetic newcomer with a love of the field. I appreciate your consideration, and look forward to meeting with you.
>
> Very truly yours,

Thank-You Letter for an Interview

After an interview, a thank-you letter gives you the opportunity to shine and differentiate yourself from the pack. It provides you a chance to sell yourself again and to focus the interviewer on key points. Here you can highlight some of the talking points from the interview, say something important you might have omitted, correct any missteps, and once again demonstrate your enthusiasm for the company and the position.

We are old-fashioned enough to believe that a letter rather than an e-mail is the appropriate form for a thank-you note, although in some circumstances, an e-mail could be appropriate. Some people send an e-mail immediately following an interview and a letter the next day.

Send a thank-you letter even if you have decided not to take the job. Even these letters should not be perfunctory; you never know when your path might cross the interviewer's again. Relationships are an important part of any business, and you don't want to burn any bridges.

Dear Mr. Greene,

Thank you very much for taking so much time out of your very hectic schedule to discuss the editorial assistant position in the juvenile division. Your enthusiasm for the books you publish is infectious, and greatly reinforced my desire to work with you and Kids Pub. My long-term goal—as you know—is to write young adult fiction, and what better way to learn than by working with one of the preeminent children's book publishers.

DID YOU KNOW?

You may interview with more than one person, often someone from human resources, but also others in various positions or departments. We recommend you send a thank you to anyone you met individually. Depending on the nature of your meeting, the note can be brief, but it should refer to something specific to your discussion with that person. If you met with people in a group, a letter to each is not essential, but your thank you to the decisionmaker should include a word of thanks to the others you met.

You mentioned that the administrative tasks that your role as editorial director demands take valuable time away from cultivating new authors and providing editorial input. I am confident that I could help remove some of that burden because I would bring to the position not only my enthusiasm for your publishing program but also my organizational and time management skills. Of necessity, I completed my bachelor's degree in three and a half years, achieving dean's list, while working 20 hours a week in the campus bookstore. When I began college, these were skills I didn't know I possessed, but necessity taught valuable lessons, and I know I could help you get through the black hole of paperwork, scheduling, and other routine tasks.

As to the editorial side of the job, the excellent publishing program at New York University grounded me in the techniques and terminology, and I got my feet wet in the real world of juvenile publishing when I interned in the marketing department of Little People's Press last summer.

Thank you again for the time you spent with me. I enjoyed meeting you, and I hope I will have the opportunity to contribute to the expansion of your young adult list.

Sincerely,

SIMPLY STATED

- Always write a thank-you letter.
  - Be personal, enthusiastic, and interested.
- Mail your letter within one day of the interview.
- Use high-quality stationery with personal letterhead.

THANK YOU FOR A JOB OFFER

Whether you decide to accept or turn down a job offer, you should respond to the person making the hiring decision, as well as the person from human resources if that's the person who notifies you of the decision. When you accept an offer, make sure you state the job title in your letter.

Accepting a Job Offer

Dear Mr. Jablonski,

Thank you so much for your offer to join Turner & Turner, Salamander & Clark as a paralegal. I look forward to receiving the official offer and employment agreement from Ms. Keyser.

I look forward to joining you and the rest of your team on the seventeenth.

Sincerely,

Declining a Job Offer

Dear Ms. Gonzales,

I very much enjoyed meeting you and the others last week, and wanted to thank you again for the informative and interesting time we spent together.

The opportunity at Richland is exciting and challenging, but I have decided to accept an offer from Stansfield, which does not involve relocation at this time.

Again, many thanks for the generous offer.

Sincerely,

RESIGNATION

People leave a job for a variety of reasons: because they are unhappy with it or with their supervisor; because they are relocating; because there was nowhere further to go; or because they receive an offer too good to refuse.

Most people resign in a face-to-face meeting with the person to whom they report. Even so, it's important to put your resignation in writing as well. Regardless of your reason for leaving, your conversation and your letter should be brief: Give the details (such as the date), say something positive (even if you are thrilled to be going), and offer assistance during the transition. Once again, the adage to burn no bridges applies. You never know when your old boss might join your new firm, or when you might need a reference.

The resignation can take the form of a memo or a letter.

> Subject: Resignation
>
> As we discussed this morning, I will be resigning from the company effective December 3. The opportunity offered me to head the accounts payable department at another firm was too good to pass up.
>
> I will always be grateful for the opportunities Smith & Jones has given me. As you know, I started as a clerk six years ago, and with your support rose to assistant manager. I could not have done it without you.
>
> I will, of course, do all I can during the transition period to make it as easy as possible for someone to pick up where I leave off and will prepare a transition memo advising you of the status of any outstanding issues.

THE JOB SEARCH—ONLINE

The number of e-recruiters online—general sites, industry-specific sites, newspaper and trade magazine help-wanted listings, college and university sites, and company websites (some even allow you to complete an application form online)—are proliferating.

All of these online resources should figure in your job search. Some sites let you upload your entire resume and cover letter. Other sites let you post only a brief version of your cover letter. Few sites allow you to customize your cover letter to the specific job, so whether it's a full-length letter or just a summary, it's important to focus on your key selling points. For a full cover letter, you can adapt the cover letters from this chapter.

E-Cover Letter (Sometimes Called a *Comment*)

> I have been in the children's clothing business for the past five years, most recently with Boys & Girls Together, where I am chief designer and manager of the girls' design division.

As my resume indicates, with a staff of eight designers and three assistants, I spearheaded the expansion of the line from a two-season dress line to one that now includes everything from outerwear to underwear as well as play, school, and dress-up clothes. Under my direction, sales of the girls' division grew from $20 million to over $100 million.

I am ready for another challenge and welcome the opportunity to meet with you to explore ways in which my skills can be applied to your needs.

As with e-mail, it's best to upload a plain-text version of your resume. Create one and save it so you can use it on different sites as well as in e-mails.

Personnel Matters
Say It Right

If you are a small businessperson, a human resources manager, or a department head, you will likely find yourself writing to

- acknowledge resumes
- accept and reject applicants
- request and provide references (see Chapter 11)
- praise, remediate, and terminate employees

Many of these communications are difficult to write, and many have legal ramifications. All must be carefully worded.

THE HIRING PROCESS

Acknowledging Resumes

Human resources professionals and some managers regularly receive unsolicited resumes. Acknowledge them, if only by a form letter; however, unless you really intend to follow up, don't say or imply that you will. Not only is it bad manners, but it inevitably generates follow-up calls and letters from the applicant.

Response to an Unsolicited Resume

Dear Applicant,

Thank you for sending us your resume. As you may know, we have no openings in your area of expertise at this time. It is our policy to keep requests on file for six months. If you do not hear from us, it means that we still do not have an opening for someone with your qualifications.

We appreciate your interest in Tri-State.

Sincerely,

Response to a Solicited Resume

Sometimes you receive so many responses to an ad that you cannot immediately respond with an invitation to an interview or with a rejection. In such cases, it is appropriate to indicate that you will get back to the applicant after you have reviewed his letter and resume.

Dear Mr. Jessup,

Thank you for responding to our ad in the *Wall Street Journal* for an account executive in our bond department. We are reviewing all of the resumes with the manager of that department and will get back to you within the next ten days.

We appreciate your interest in Bonds Unlimited, and regret any inconvenience this delay may cause.

Sincerely,

Making a Job Offer

Often, job offers and acceptances are verbal, and followed by negotiation of salary, benefits, and so on. Once the details have been agreed upon, a formal acceptance letter follows.

Some companies have formal employment agreements, signed by both parties. An acceptance letter, while not so formal, carries legal weight. For this reason, some firms use a template reviewed by their attorney. Acceptance letters generally tell the new employee the date of hire and job title; the salary and how often payment is made; and the length of the qualifying period, if any, before the employee is entitled to benefits.

If the letter is the initial job offer, it is a good idea to give the applicant some stipulated amount of time in which to consider the offer and reply. Salary, benefits, and other issues should have been made clear during the interview process.

Dear Ms. Kane,

Marbury & Madison are pleased to offer you the position of Director, Sales and Marketing, to begin on July 5, 2008. The base salary is $163,500; payment to be made bimonthly (26 times a year on the 15th and 30th of each month). You are also eligible for a bonus based on achievement of certain goals, which are described in detail in the bonus plan enclosed.

Employee benefits are described in detail in the material enclosed; please read it carefully. In summary, health insurance, life insurance, and disability benefits will begin three months from date of employment, and you will be entitled to three weeks (15 business days) of vacation each year for the first four years (accrued at the rate of 1.25 days per month). You may participate in our 401(k) as well as our stock option plan from the date of employment.

Please return the attached documents to us no later than June 25th, and don't hesitate to call if you have any questions. If not, we look forward to seeing you again on the 5th of July. An orientation session is scheduled for 9 A.M. in the human resources office on the 25th floor. We look forward to welcoming you then.

Sincerely,

Turning Down an Applicant

Accepting an applicant is easy; rejecting one can be hard, particularly when you liked the applicant, but, for one reason or another, the fit wasn't right.

After Meeting the Candidate

Dear Ms. Santos,

I enjoyed meeting you last week to discuss the creative director's position. Your portfolio is very impressive. I especially liked the campaign you designed for the RetroRedRoadster.

As you know, we sell our products business to business rather than direct to consumer, an area in which you have no direct experience. For this reason, we have decided to hire an applicant with more B-to-B experience. Although I am confident that with your background and talent you would have learned the special skills required to market in this area, we are a small firm and must "hit the ground running."

Thank you again for coming in and sharing your ideas.

Sincerely,

In most cases, however, when rejecting an applicant, the less-is-more approach applies.

Dear Mr. Touloukian,

Tom Jones, Emma Lazarus, and I enjoyed our discussion with you last week about career opportunities with Tompkins Travel & Tours. While your credentials as a tour guide are impressive, we have decided to go with a candidate who has also had managerial experience.

Again, many thanks for your interest in Tompkins; we wish you all the best in your career.

Sincerely,

If You Have Not Met the Candidate

Dear Mr. Stoppard,

Thank you for sending your resume in response to our advertisement for a sales trainee. We regret to inform you that we have filled the position with another candidate.

We received many responses to the ad, reviewed all of them very carefully, and selected the candidate whose experience and career goals best meshed with our plans for the future.

Again, thank you for your interest. We wish you success in your career.

Sincerely,

COMMUNICATING WITH EMPLOYEES

Praising an Employee

There are many ways to praise an employee: a face-to-face *thank you* or *congratulations, you did a great job*, an e-mail (if you're not in the same office), a bonus, a gift, and so on. A memo to file and/or one to the entire company or department (this can be an e-mail) is also welcome.

Praising the Employee Directly

Subject: Congratulations

The annual figures are in, and I wanted to be the first to thank you for the fabulous job you did this year. All year, your numbers were coming in ahead of pace, but we never thought you could do what you did last quarter—you nearly doubled your sales goals.

To show our appreciation, we are sending you a gift certificate for two, for a ten-day cruise in the Caribbean. Enjoy it; you deserve it.

Praising the Employee to the Staff

Subject: Employee of the Week—Sara Parker

Please join the management team and me in congratulating Sara on the excellent job she did getting the word out about the new fall Fashion for Pooches line-up. She even managed to get us top-of-the-fold in the Style Section in the *New York Times* last week. No mean feat!

We'll be toasting Sara on Friday at 4 P.M. with a small wine and cheese celebration in the fourth-floor meeting room. We hope you'll join us.

Memo to Human Resources File

Subject: Exceptional Performance

After last week's hurricane, Marissa was one of a handful of people living close enough to the hospital to come in without taking public transportation. Although she was not scheduled to be on duty for another two days, she arrived—without being called—and remained in the ICU for 36 hours until a sufficient number of replacement nurses were able to return.

THE FIRING PROCESS

Most companies have written policies and procedures to document all the steps a manager or human resources person must take when an employee's work or work habits have fallen off. Most are aimed at correcting the behavior, if possible, but they also provide documentation in the event the decision is made to terminate the employee.

Never use e-mail to document an employee's behavior, give a warning to an employee, or terminate an employee. Such information is confidential, and e-mails can too easily fall into the wrong person's inbox.

SIMPLY STATED

When reprimanding an employee:

- Focus on the specific issue.
- Avoid generalizations.
- Avoid emotional language.
- Focus on the specific actions needed to correct the problem.

Never forget, you are not an analyst or member of the clergy.

Documenting Warnings

Generally, the process starts with a series of verbal conversations discussing the problem with the employee. You should document an employee's behavior, the conversation, and the action you took with a memo to file; and you should write it immediately, so that the conversation is fresh in your mind. If necessary, these documents will form the basis for a written reprimand or a performance review.

Memo to File after a Verbal Reprimand

Subject: Conversation re Goals

I met with Dwayne this morning at about 11 A.M. on October 3, 2007, to discuss why he thought he had not achieved his goals for the past two months in terms of either number of cold calls made or actual orders placed. August was down 5% and September down 8.5%. I told him that I thought missing one month was a fluke but I was concerned since this was two consecutive months (and the numbers had fallen from month to month) at a hot time of year. (Note: None of the others missed their goals in either month and some exceeded them by as much as 10%.)

Dwayne said he had been having some personal problems; that his mother was ill and he had been distracted by his concern for her as well as having to arrange for caregivers when he was working. I expressed concern, suggested he might want to take some vacation time, or take advantage of the Employee Assistance Plan or the Family Leave Act. He indicated this was not necessary, apologized, and assured me that his mother was improving and that he believed he had found excellent help.

We agreed to review his performance in two weeks and then, again, at the end of the month.

Written Reprimand

Subject: Failure to Meet Goals

As we discussed in our meetings on October 3, October 17, and October 31, your sales goals—number of cold calls made and numbers of orders taken—have not been met since August, and each month is worse that the one preceding it—August was down 5%, September down 8.5%, and October 9%. Tracking your November goals against one-week results shows no sign of improvement. Sales are running at about 9% below expectations.

I know that your mother has been ill, and, of course, you have my personal sympathies, but I have suggested options that you have chosen not to take. Therefore, unless there is immediate improvement as demonstrated by meeting your goals for November, remedial action—either a leave of absence without pay, or termination—may be taken.

Final Warning

Subject: Final Warning: Failure to Meet Goals

This memo follows up on my written reprimand dated November 7. Once again, sales are tracking below goals, this time just above 9%. We have offered several options that you have chosen not to take to help you through a difficult period.

These results are unacceptable. Therefore, unless there is immediate improvement as demonstrated by meeting your goals for December, remedial action—either a leave of absence without pay, or termination—will be taken.

Termination of Employment for Cause

Subject: Termination of Employment

This will confirm our conversation this morning. Effective January 18, your employment with Hammond Industries is terminated. The reasons were documented in conversations and memos to you dated November 7 and December 7 regarding your failure to meet sales goals since August 2007.

Please contact Louisa Marsalis in human resources about continuation of benefits, severance pay, etc.

Thank you for your past efforts, and best wishes for your future endeavors.

Termination of Employment for No Fault of the Employee

Sometimes you must lay someone off because the company has merged, or relocated, or is going through difficult financial times, or a myriad of other reasons. Often many people are laid off simultaneously. In either case, either individually or as a group, they are given verbal notice and explanation, which is then followed by a formal notice.

> Subject: Branch Closing
>
> Further to our meeting this morning, your employment with Cowboy Country will be terminated effective May 19.
>
> As you know, Cowboy Country was purchased in March by Smith & Western Apparel, who has a large Dallas operation. They have determined that increasing the size of your department does not fit their current business model. This does not in any way reflect the excellent work the Dallas branch has done over the past five years since it opened.
>
> You will each be receiving information about relocation possibilities within the Smith & Western group as well as information on COBRA and other benefits to which you are entitled, severance pay, unemployment insurance, and so on. We have hired a firm to help you with your job search, and we will, of course, provide references. Bill Jennings and Marva Payne in human resources will be scheduling individual meetings with each of you to discuss these and any other questions you may have, and to provide you with benefit and other information packets.
>
> Thank you for your past service and for your assistance during the transition to new ownership.

CHAPTER ELEVEN

References, Recommendations, and Introductions

Making Connections

According to the *Random House Unabridged Dictionary*, a reference is "a statement, usually written, as to a person's character, abilities, etc." and a recommendation is "a letter or the like recommending a person or thing." Is there any real difference? Frankly, not very much.

In everyday terms, a reference is associated with employment whereas a recommendation is associated with academics. The word *reference* may also refer to a *character* reference, such as one might be asked to give when someone is applying for club membership or purchasing a co-op apartment. Letters of introduction are a type of recommendation, but not necessarily for a position (although they may lead to one); they carry less formal weight, and the information they provide is much more general. They might be used to introduce someone to a friend, a customer, a client, or even an acquaintance.

Whatever you call it, giving a reference, recommendation, or introduction has become more and more complicated in our increasingly litigious society. Where once they were strictly confidential, and sometimes still are, more and more often that is not the case. Frequently, the person asking for the recommendation expects a copy, even though you may have been asked to send it directly to the person who requested it. It can be awkward not to provide a copy. In any case, the institution itself may provide the person with a copy, so it's best to assume the person will see it.

In an effort to avoid legal problems, which can be expensive, some companies now have strict name-rank-and-serial-number policies; that is, they only *verify* (not provide) information such as dates of employment, salary, and position. Often these companies do not let managers provide even this verification, but insist that all requests go through the appropriate human resources manager.

Verbal references are somewhat easier; after all, there is no written record for the person to see. Nevertheless, the same legal considerations apply.

DID YOU KNOW?

Etiquette dictates that you ask permission before giving someone's name as a reference. Etiquette also permits you to refuse to give a reference if you haven't been asked. However, as a former employer, manager, or supervisor you may be named on an application and be contacted without the applicant's knowledge.

That said, if you are a manager or a teacher or a professor or sometimes even just a friend, you may be asked to provide a reference. Just because you are asked, don't think that you have to say yes. Like some companies, some people make it a policy not to give references; others only give them to certain people or in certain circumstances.

ASKING FOR A REFERENCE

Depending on your relationship, you can ask for a reference either by telephone or by e-mail. However, for a number of reasons (company policy, primarily), not everyone can agree to provide one or, for personal reasons, feels comfortable giving one.

When we ask someone to act as a reference, we do so assuming the person will give us a great reference—or at least a good one. You can help make sure that your references will be good by letting the person know the position you are seeking, the type of company, and so on. It will give the person time to think about you, and plan what to say so that they can emphasize those things that are key to the particular position.

It will also help avoid an uncomfortable situation; for example, a manager who thought you were a great sales rep might not think you are experienced enough to be a regional manager. To avoid discomfort to your reference or risk getting a less than stellar review, it is a wise—and polite—policy to test the waters by asking first and providing information about the position.

SIMPLY STATED

When asking someone to give you a reference, make sure it will be a good one. Look for clues:

- **Is the person enthusiastic?**
- **Is the person hesitant?**
- **Does the person seem reluctant to agree?**

A General Request to a Former Employer

Dear Jason,

I would appreciate your assistance with my job search. I am seeking a position in the hospitality industry, preferably with an international hotel chain.

May I have your permission to use you as a reference? If you agree, I will let you know whenever I give your name to a prospective employer, and fill you in on the details of the company and the position for which I am applying.

Many thanks for your help.

Sincerely,

A Request about a Specific Position

Subject: May I use you as a reference?

I've been interviewing with Sam Spade, who runs a business called The Private Eye, a boutique line of fashion eyewear. He has seven stores in the metropolitan area and wants to expand to San Francisco. As you know, I've always wanted to relocate to the Coast and this seems like a perfect opportunity.

I would be responsible for finding the location, getting it up and running, managing the first store, and then expanding following the model he used in NYC but adapting it to a California sensibility.

Would you mind talking to Sam about my work with you at Eyes on the Piazza; in particular, the launch of the mall stores? If you are unable to do it, I'll understand, but I'd be grateful if you'd get back to me by Tuesday because I told Sam I'd have a list for him when we meet again on Wednesday. Many thanks.

To a Friend

Subject: I'm buying a co-op; will you be my reference?

Hi, Sharon,

I've finally done it. I've made an offer on a one-bedroom on the Upper West Side. Negotiations are over, and all that's left is the dreaded meeting with the co-op board, which is scheduled for March 1. They want two character references, and since we've known each other practically all our lives, I thought who better than you. Plus, you are such a pillar of the community, I think it would be impressive if it came on the letterhead of your prestigious law firm.

You can tell I'm excited and I'd be so grateful if you could do this for me (only teasing about the letterhead, although it would knock their socks off!). E-mail me if you get a chance, or I'll call on Wednesday. Many, many thanks.

DECLINING TO PROVIDE A REFERENCE

Unless it's against company policy to provide references, this can be a hard message to send. The best advice is to be as short, simple, and truthful as possible without going into details.

Subject: Reference

Madeline,

After considerable thought, I have concluded that I cannot provide the reference you requested. When you worked for me at the EPA you had an entry-level position. Although your work then was excellent, the position you are being considered for at the Watershed Protection Agency is at a much higher level, and, because I have no direct knowledge of your experience over the past five years, I would not be comfortable providing a reference. I hope you understand.

With best wishes for your success,

PROVIDING REFERENCES

References range from moderate to wildly enthusiastic depending on the reference-giver's analysis of the person and his or her ability to perform the particular job. References are most often letters, but if you the request is e-mailed to you, an e-mail reply—with an attachment—is acceptable unless you were asked to mail your response.

A Good Reference

Dear Ms. Hughes,

Lucille Rappaport reported to me for three years; she was a children's book librarian and I was chief librarian at the main branch of the Titusville Library.

Lucille's responsibilities included selection and acquisition of print as well as electronic media, which she did very well, making wise decisions despite budgetary constraints. Lucille was knowledgeable, hardworking, and very good with the children, who especially enjoyed the weekly story hour, as well as with her staff of three.

I recommend her for the head children's librarian opening described in your letter.

Sincerely,

An Enthusiastic Reference

Sometimes you are asked to provide a general all-purpose reference that a person can use whenever he or she applies for a job.

To Whom It May Concern:

Boyd Worthington and I worked together at Grimes & Grimes for nearly eight years. For the last five of those years, he reported directly to me. Boyd was a development editor, and when he reported to me, I was an executive editor, and later an editorial director.

Boyd is multitalented. He writes well, understands how to help an author build the right book for the intended market, can analyze and evaluate proposals, and has the ability to work with editors and marketers. His ability to analyze competition and contribute to market research not only enhanced his ability to edit, but also made his comments more informative at publishing committee meetings. His writing skills were invaluable.

Boyd's exceptional people skills are a strong asset when working with colleagues, and invaluable when it comes to working with authors. In addition, his flexibility and willingness to pitch in when necessary add to the strong contribution he makes.

No one who hires him will be disappointed. Should you need additional information, please feel free to call or e-mail.

Sincerely,

A Recommendation for Graduate School

To Sara Siddons, Graduate School of Arts & Sciences:

I have known Gloria Shahin for about six years. Gloria reported to me when I was the art director and she was an illustrator at Stieglitz & Kahlo Advertising Agency.

Her responsibilities included concept and design of all illustration associated with a product, including

- package design
- print media
- poster art

Gloria always performed well in all of these and other tasks that were thrown at her during a very hectic time in the agency's history. She always maintained an air of quiet control, was in command of her material, and had excellent relationships with colleagues at all levels as well as with the clients with whom she worked.

Since then our paths have diverged as she had gone on to work as a freelancer, then later joined another agency, and then on to graduate school at the State University. I have formed my own firm and have been fortunate enough to employ Gloria from time to time on a freelance basis.

I enthusiastically recommend her to your program knowing that she will do well in whatever activity she pursues.

Please don't hesitate to contact me again should you need additional information.

Sincerely,

THANK YOU FOR YOUR REFERENCE

Dear Mr. Kazanjian,

Thank you once again for allowing me to use your name in applying for the job at Hollings, Surhesh & Trevalyan. The competition was keen and I gather from a number of comments that were made during the several interviews that I had with them that the references I received were influential in their decisionmaking process.

I will be starting there in two weeks, and can't tell you how pleased I am to have this opportunity. Thank you for your help in making it possible.

Sincerely,

INTRODUCTIONS

Introductions are a formal way to acquaint two people you know with one another. Although far less common than they once were, they are used in both business and social situations or business-social situations, and are a form of networking. You might write such a letter when someone is moving to another state or country or to facilitate an interview for information. When this type of letter was more common, the person about whom the letter was written might have hand-delivered it after arranging an appointment; today, it's far more likely that you'd send the letter by mail or e-mail.

Introducing Business Colleagues

Subject: Favor

My colleague, Joe Stein, has been promoted and is transferring to our Boston office. He's originally from Santa Barbara and moved to Chicago to work for me about three years ago. We've become great friends as well as business colleagues, and I am going to miss him both professionally and personally.

It turns out he knows no one in Boston except a couple of people from the office, and although I'm sure that they'll give him a warm welcome, I thought you and he would hit it off. He's an avid sports fan and I know how you feel about the Patriots and the Sox—maybe you'll be able to convert him. Actually, I think you and he have much in common and would enjoy one another's company. I've given him your numbers and told him to look you up once he's settled in.

Let me know if I'm right. In the meantime, hope you and the family are well and that you'll be coming to Chicago soon. The Blues festival is coming up and we all had such a great time last year.

Best,

Facilitating an Interview for Information

Dear Norma,

My nephew just graduated from the School of Industrial Design at The Art Institute of Philadelphia. I'm biased of course, but I think he's a bright young man, far more levelheaded than I was at his age, and interested in pursuing a career in designing housewares and other products for everyday use. He's also quite personable and I think you'd enjoy meeting him.

He wants to attend graduate school but would like to take some time to get his feet wet working in the industry. With your experience in the field, I thought you'd be the perfect person to give him advice. Can you spare a half hour to meet with him? I'd be so grateful. Let me know if it's okay and I'll give him your name and number.

Best regards,

CHAPTER **TWELVE**

Replies

Answering the Mail

We have already reviewed how to respond to letters of complaint, requests for employment and references, and many others in the chapters dealing with those topics. In this chapter, we will examine how to handle such seemingly simple but essential things as

- acknowledgments
- apologies
- confirmations
- follow-ups
- invitations
- referrals
- refusals

Reply letters fall into two categories. The first are letters that may require only a line or two in response, but often in a day spent in dealing with larger issues, we neglect the little ones and inadvertently damage our own or our firm's reputation.

SIMPLY STATED

The keys to properly handling routine matters are

- responding promptly, in a succinct manner
- being courteous
- following through, if necessary

In the second category are those letters that require greater thought and attention, but which may arrive at an inopportune moment. Rather than let these letters pile up on your desk, review them quickly, pass along those on which you can delegate the initial response, and/or design a form letter that you can personalize, if necessary, to initiate the first step in what might be a long-term dialogue or that might eliminate the need to go any further. As always, if you commit to responding more fully later, be sure to do so.

Close the door to further correspondence if you have no interest in pursuing the subject. By failing to do this, you may be trying not to hurt someone's feelings, but you are wasting your time as well as theirs.

ACKNOWLEDGMENTS

Most, but not all, correspondence that requires an acknowledgment comes by mail from someone outside the company and should therefore be acknowledged by letter. However, if the writer has e-mailed or suggested that you may respond by e-mail, you can feel free to do so.

Request for Sponsorship

Dear Ms. Stempel,

Thank you for your invitation to sponsor a table at the National Arts Club Annual Masked Ball. The Club is a worthy cause and the event sounds as if it would be great fun.

As you can imagine, as a producer of photographic paper, we receive many requests from many excellent arts organizations. At the beginning of the year, we review our commitments for the subsequent 18 months, and then quarterly review new requests. Our next review will be in September, after which we will get back to you with our decision.

Yours truly,

Receipt of Request for Proposal

This is a good example of the kind of personalized form acknowledgment that provides additional information that essentially qualifies the recipient; that is, it tells the potential client the basis on which you will proceed. If these terms are not acceptable, there's no need to go into further detail or prepare an agreement.

Dear Mr. Regan,

Thank you for your letter soliciting an RFP for the construction of a Japanese garden, bridges, walkways, ponds, and waterfall at your new corporate headquarters in Englewood Cliffs.

In order to perform the high-quality work for which Kyoto Gardens is known—as exemplified by the gardens you cite in your request—we send a team consisting of a landscape architect, a horticulturalist, an engineer, a surveyor, and their assistants to the site.

They spend a minimum of three days on site familiarizing themselves with all aspects of the terrain. They then create the preliminary sketches and cost estimates. Our minimum fee up to this point is $50,000 payable half on signing our contract and half on submission of sketches and estimates. We will submit receipts for travel and expenses incurred. Based on our current schedule, we could have a team on site in early March.

If this is acceptable, please let us know and we will send a contract.

Sincerely,

APOLOGIES

People make mistakes; it's inevitable. When you've made a mistake, don't try to duck responsibility or blame the other guy, and don't pretend it will go away if you ignore it. Most mistakes are small infractions that can be remedied if handled promptly and well; if not, small mistakes can grow into large unwieldy brouhahas.

The exception that proves the rule: If the mistake has legal ramifications, consult with your attorney and/or the company's attorney before saying anything at all.

Apology for Missing a Deadline

Here it's good to face the music as soon as you realize that you are going to be late. Telling your client or colleagues at the last minute can leave them in a bind, whereas if you give them warning, they may be able to get you some help or reschedule if necessary.

Subject: Proposal

Logan,

We are running about a week behind on the proposal for Smith Sons, Inc. I know it is due on Tuesday, August 8, but it looks like we won't complete compiling the data until Friday. I should have realized that the data would not be available sooner, and should not have told you I could have the proposal on the eighth. I have authorized overtime, so we should be able to pick up a few days, but it looks like the earliest we'll have it to you is Thursday, August 10. I will give you a daily update.

I am sorry for the inconvenience I know this causes you and your department. Believe me, I'll check all the facts before I make a similar promise again.

Apology for Missing an Appointment

Dear Lisa,

I am so sorry I missed our meeting. What you must think of me! As you know, I was on a whirlwind trip, and it looks like I did not transfer all my appointments from my desktop to my BlackBerry.

Not showing up for lunch is unforgivable, although I do hope you will let me atone in a small way with this gift certificate to Shalimar for you and a guest.

CONFIRMATIONS

Unlike acknowledgments, you may confirm something—often an appointment or a reservation—with people both inside and outside the organization. E-mails are often appropriate when you are confirming a meeting or a reservation at a restaurant or hotel or other travel plans (in fact, e-tickets have become ubiquitous).

Hotel Reservation

Subject: Reservation

Steve,

This confirms the reservations we discussed for the three double rooms with king-size beds, for Cheryl and Arthur Tarkington, Naomi and Ari Schwartz, and Irene and Mark Castle, who will be arriving on May 10 and departing on May 17.

Please provide each room with fruit, chocolate, and flower baskets on their arrival. All are guests of Talent Associates and all charges, including room service and restaurant and bar bills, should be charged to our account.

Many thanks as always for your help in making our guests feel welcome.

Order Confirmation

An order placed via the Internet is acknowledged immediately on the website or by e-mail. An e-mailed order is typically acknowledged by e-mail, while one sent by mail is typically acknowledged by mail—often in the form of an invoice. If an order is placed over the telephone, the order taker generally provides a confirmation number and details orally. (Sometimes shipping confirmation follows once the item has shipped.)

E-Mail Confirming an Order

Subject: Dinnerware Deluxe: Order Confirmation #36608188

Thank you for your order.

Ship to:
Suna Moomjy
222 Sydney Ct.
Kingston, NY 12401

Please print this email for your records. We're here to help. If you need any assistance with your order, please contact Customer Service at 1-800-967-0006.

Order Number:
36608188
Order Date:
9/11/2008

Items	Shipping Via	Qty	Price	Total	Gift Box	Availability
Onyx Mug SKU 111-000	Standard Shipping	6	$5.95	$35.70	No	Available
Onyx Creamer SKU 111-007	Standard Shipping	1	$5.95	$ 5.95	No	Available
Order Total:		Total Merchandise:		$41.65		
		Total Shipping:		$ 5.25		
		Total Taxes:		$ 2.50		
		Total Charge:		**$49.40**		

Letter Confirming an Order

This letter is going to a regular customer, hence the informality.

Dear Sally,

Thank you for your purchase order #297-72 for copy paper:

3 cartons	$8\frac{1}{2} \times 11''$	bright white
2 cartons	$8\frac{1}{2} \times 11''$	canary yellow
1 carton	$8\frac{1}{2} \times 11''$	bright white

We will deliver it on Tuesday, August 23, between 9 A.M. and 5 P.M. and will charge the items to your account.

As always, it is a pleasure doing business with you.

Cordially,

FOLLOW-UPS

There are myriad reasons for following up on something. A confirmation, for example, is a kind of follow-up, as is a memo sent after a meeting summing up the points that were made and specifying who was to do what. A follow-up may be sent to people inside or outside the organization. E-mails are more and more common for this purpose, but internally you might choose a memo; externally a letter is fine.

DID YOU KNOW?

It's always helpful when asking someone to do additional or last-minute work to explain the reason for it.

Subject: Sales Figures

Vanessa,

Just a quick note to remind you that third-quarter figures are due on Tuesday and that we are meeting on Thursday at 3 with the other members of the management committee.

At that meeting, I'd also like you to cover the forecast for the fourth quarter, both actual orders on hand and those that have been promised. I'm not concerned with the details of every order for small quantities, although I would like your best estimate of the total quantity, but would like to know the specifics of any order over $2,500.

We've had production problems, as you know, with a few major items and, now that we are back on track, we may need to take steps to meet the demand for them and expedite manufacturing so we can have them in the warehouse when we need them.

INVITATIONS

An invitation to business social events—from someone inside or outside your organization—is a request that needs to be handled carefully. Often, you may not want to attend a holiday party, a company picnic, or dinner at a client's or your boss's home, but, although purely social invitations may be optional, business invitations to social events really are not optional, and unless you have a good reason for not attending, it's important to say yes. Such events are opportunities to cement relationships and enhance your career; not going can have the opposite effect. If you have to turn down an invitation, make sure you have a good reason for doing so.

If your spouse is invited to an event, he or she should attend (again, unless there's a very good reason not to go).

Accepting an Invitation from the Boss

John,

Cathy and I would be delighted to join you for doubles and brunch at your club on Sunday, September 3.

Thank you so much for including us. Tell Barbara we are looking forward to seeing her and thank her for us as well.

Turning Down an Invitation from a Client

Virginia,

I wish I could join you and the others for golf next weekend; I had such a great time the last time we golfed. However, I must be in Basel for the entire week at the annual watch and jewelry convention. It opens on Saturday the 3rd and closes on the 10th, and we will be flying home on Sunday. Any other time, I'd love to go. Please think of me the next time you are putting a foursome together.

Wishing you luck!

REFERRALS

The most common form of business referral comes when an inquiry goes to the wrong person in an organization (some people automatically write to the president) or you decide to delegate the response to someone else on your staff or give it to someone in another department or division to handle. The purpose of the response is to acknowledge the inquiry and let the inquirer know who will be handling it.

Another type of referral is a request about where to find a particular product or service.

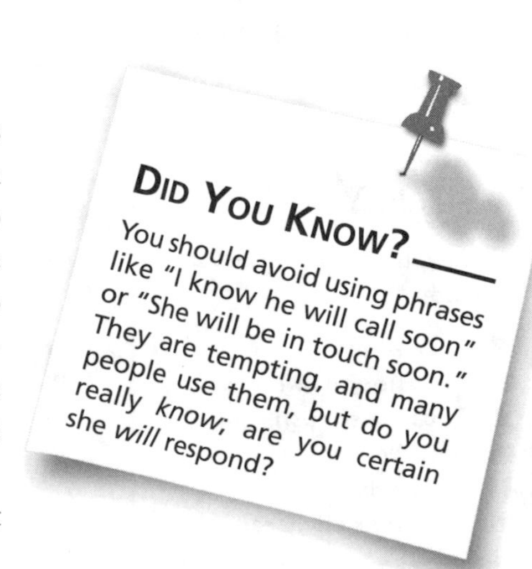

Passing an Inquiry along to a Colleague

Dear Ms. McHugh,

Thank you for your letter requesting information about our new skin care products. Svensen & Spensor, located at 236 Fifth Avenue, distribute them in your area. I have passed your letter on to Inge Svensen, who is extremely knowledgeable about all our products, and have asked her to contact you directly.

Thank you for your interest in Soft-to-Touch moisturizers and creams.

Very truly yours,

Recommending a Service

Subject: Referral

Stan,

Yes, I do know a very good printer in your area who can do the kind of high-quality, short-run printing you need. My contact there is Martin (Marty) Pilsudski; his e-mail address is mpilsuds@printer.com, phone, 666-966-3672. He's a great guy and can help with advice about paper and cover stock. He can also do the design and layout work if you need that. Use my name.

Good luck with the project!

REFUSALS

It's hard to say no to a request in personal or business life. Still, it is sometimes not only necessary but also unavoidable, as when you have to reject a job applicant or turn down a request for credit.

> **SIMPLY STATED**
>
> When you have to refuse a request,
>
> - *Do be direct.*
> - *Don't use the word no.*
> - *Do tell the truth.*
> - *Don't be emotional.*
> - *Do be brief.*
> - *Don't make it personal.*

Turning Down Requests

Sometimes no matter how persuasive a request is, you simply can't agree to it. Still, you would prefer to retain the client's (or employee's or colleague's) goodwill. A response to a letter of complaint is a good example (see Chapter 5). Clearly, you want to keep the customer, but you may not be able to satisfy her desire to make a return without a receipt. The key is not to appear arbitrary and unreasonable, and the best way to do this is to give an explanation—not an excuse and not an apology (unless one is called for)—for your decision, and, where possible, to offer an alternative. The other person may not like the result, but should understand your decision.

Denying a Hiring Request

Subject: Increased Staff

Sam,

You made a great case for why you want to hire two new accounting clerks. As you know, there is a hiring freeze throughout the company, and if I grant this exception, I know I would have similar requests on my desk as soon as word got out.

We will be reviewing the freeze in July. If business conditions turn around, as we hope they will, we can review your request at that time.

I appreciate the effort that you and your team are putting in, but I am sure you will understand why we can't make exceptions at this time.

Turning Down a Request for an Interview

Dear Mr. Grolier,

Ms. Messina passed along your request to interview me for the *Times Picayune* about the role of the insurance industry in handling Hurricane Katrina-related claims. Right now, our association is still gathering data from our members and, as you know, Congress is investigating the matter. For these reasons, it would be premature for me to speak to this issue.

Sincerely,

CHAPTER **THIRTEEN**

Requests

The Power to Persuade

In earlier chapters, we talked about specific requests, such as a request for an information interview. When you think about it, many of the letters we send and receive are requests. A resume cover letter is a type of request. So is a letter of complaint. In this chapter, we will review a variety of requests that are the daily fare of most business lives, including requests for

- a quote
- a sample
- product information
- terms of sale
- an order

All of these and others are requests to someone outside of the company for which you work.

Other requests are made to people inside the company, for example, to

- attend a meeting
- provide information
- comment on a report or a situation

Some requests, like favors or invitations, are sent to people both inside and outside an organization. Some requests are easy to make and easy to answer; others require considerable tact, diplomacy, and frequently great powers of persuasion as well. Which of the many requests you receive each day will you respond to? There are the things you *must* do, but then there are all those other things you're asked to do. Sure, if the boss is asking, you may not have much choice, but what about requests from colleagues? How do you decide? Similarly, when you ask someone for something, does that person comply? It's not simply a question of clout; how you ask will make a difference.

In this chapter, we will show you how to respond and follow up on as well as make requests.

EASY INTERNAL REQUESTS

Most interoffice requests that once were made by memo can now be sent via e-mail.

Request for a Report

Subject: Stock Status Report

As you know, we will be meeting on April 12 to review inventory. To expedite our discussion, please distribute to all attendees no later than April 6 an Excel copy of the stock status report as of March 31, so that we can all come prepared with suggestions for reorders, returns, special offers, and so on. Thank you.

Setting Up a Lunch Date to Meet a New Client

Subject: Lunch to meet Arnold Gingrich—August 2

Yusef,

As you know, Arnold (Arnie) Gingrich is a new client. Although his company is still growing, I believe it has the potential to become a major client. His company has already received press in the *Journal* and other business publications.

Arnie is coming to town for a brief visit and will be here for only one week, from August 1–6. His schedule is quite tight, and when I suggested lunch, he indicated that August 2 worked well for him.

I know he would feel honored if the executive vice president were present. Is there any chance you can join us? As I am aware of your limited availability, I have not yet mentioned the possibility of your accompaniment.

At your convenience, please let me know if you would be available for lunch on the 2nd. I'd like to confirm with him and make a reservation at the V.I.P. room, which, as you know, books up quickly, even in the summer.

SIMPLY STATED

Straightforward requests for information/orders for products or services should

- clearly describe the product
- state when product is needed, if appropriate
- be easy to respond to

SALES-RELATED REQUESTS AND ORDERS

Today, many websites allow you to request catalogs, product information, or terms, place an order, and so on either through an e-mail generated directly from the site, by completing a form right then and there, or by accessing the catalog, brochure, or technical information online.

Not everyone, however, is comfortable providing information via the Internet or enjoys reading information online or wading through cumbersome printouts. For them—and for those who just prefer good old-fashioned hard copy to thumb through—a letter or e-mail to the company (if a special address is provided) or to a contact (if you have one) is appropriate.

E-Mail Request for Product Information

Subject: Product Information Request: Small Business Network

We are upgrading our computer system and plan to purchase 12 new computers running Vista. We want to network the computers for Internet service (we have a fiber-optic system through our telephone company) and also want to link them to three inkjet printers, two laser printers, and one color printer. Our office is approximately 3,000 square feet.

Package #LS1232, which we saw on your website, appears to include all the hardware necessary for a system of this size. We would appreciate receiving technical and price information about it and any other system you believe would work in the environment described.

We'd also like to know about warranty, repair, and support services you provide. We'd plan to be up and running in two months, and therefore would like to receive this information by return mail to the address below as quickly as possible.

Thank you.

Request for a Quote

Subject: Request for Quote

We are interested in leasing three new, current-year Mercedes-Benz S550 4MATIC Sedans, under two-year lease arrangements. We anticipate that the average annual mileage for each vehicle will be 25,000.

The cars are to be delivered to San Francisco, Chicago, and New York. We would like to begin rental in one month.

Please quote your best price to include all insurance, taxes, and maintenance, mileage overage charges, and any other expenses, as well as end-of-lease buyout information. Thank you.

Placing an Order

Dear Ms. Solares,

Thank you for your assistance. It was so good of you to leave the samples.

I have decided to purchase the wooden blinds for my home office, color #K-12. You have the measurements, but just to confirm, the window is 67″ wide × 57″ high and the blinds are to open from the bottom up rather than top down, as we discussed.

You specified that delivery would be in approximately two weeks, and quoted a price of $573.50 delivered, installed, and including tax. Enclosed is my check #237 for $300, which represents the 50% deposit you requested. The balance due after satisfactory installation is $273.50 and, as we agreed, may also be paid by check.

Please phone the number above to set up a delivery date, since I frequently travel on business. Thank you again.

Sincerely,

DIFFICULT INTERNAL REQUESTS

When something is hard to ask for, it is generally because the benefit may not be apparent to the other person or to the department or to the company. For this reason, you need to frame your request in a way that makes the benefit apparent, or at least compensates the person for the effort, and convinces him or her to act on your or the company's behalf.

Request for Promotion

Most companies set aside specific times of year during which performance evaluations are made and raises given. Most companies also have guidelines for applying for a new position inside the company. Occasionally—for example, when a new boss is hired who is unfamiliar with the fact that you were given greater and greater responsibility without a change in title or remuneration—it is appropriate to make such a request between review periods.

There are two ways to do this. One is in a short note requesting a meeting to discuss the subject, and the other is to outline your reasons in a letter or memo—not an e-mail—to your new supervisor.

Put the memo in an envelope and mark it *Confidential.*

Subject: Change in Job Status

I have worked as a junior accountant for the past two years. When I began, my responsibilities included assisting the accounting staff with financial statement preparation, month-end close, building spreadsheets, and other ad hoc projects.

During this time, I have learned a number of new skills that make me a more valuable employee, including

- posting general ledger entries
- assisting in the preparation and maintenance of general ledger
- reconciling bank accounts
- performing general ledger account reconciliations

I also worked on a number of special projects in connection with the acquisition of B&B Batteries. In addition, I am a third-year accounting major at State University, with a 3.5 GPA.

With this record and with the skills I have acquired at State, which are not yet being put to practical use, I am confident I can make a greater contribution to the company in a position with more responsibility as well as additional compensation.

I would like to meet with you at your convenience to discuss these possibilities and to fill you in further on my background and plans. Thank you for your consideration.

SIMPLY STATED

In concrete terms, inform your new boss of your

- accomplishments
- contributions
- skills and knowledge, and how these qualities have prepared you for increased responsibility

Asking Staff to Work Weekends

Subject: Volunteers for Weekend Work

As you know, the department is down two people: Casey, who is out on family leave caring for his mom, and Jennifer, who has just had a baby. That means that we have fewer hands during our busiest time of year.

I know that it's also a busy time in your personal lives, which is why I am asking for volunteers rather than setting up an arbitrary rotation. What's needed is one extra person each week between now and Christmas to staff up for the holiday rush. If you have the time, please let me know the day or days you can work during this period. Volunteers will receive prorated pay at the weekend rate, or an extra $1\frac{1}{2}$ vacation days in lieu of salary for each day worked. Vacation days may be taken between December 26, 2007, and May 1, 2008.

I have posted a sign-up sheet on the bulletin board, and I hope that each of you will be able to take at least one day. Thanks for your help in getting us over a difficult hurdle.

FAVORS

You may find yourself needing a favor from someone in or outside the organization for which you work; it may be someone you know well or someone you hardly know. Some favors—such as advice from a friend—are easy to ask for; some—like the request to a supervisor—are more difficult. In all cases, when you request a favor, it's important to explain what you want, why you have asked that particular person, and why you want or need the favor. It's equally important to offer to reciprocate (if possible), and to thank the person for her or his effort or consideration.

A Favor from a Business Acquaintance

Dear Kevin,

I wonder if you can help me locate a good but inexpensive digital camera. I know you've bought several for yourself and others.

I'd like to give them as holiday gifts to about 50 of my best customers, and, frankly, I know nothing about them. I'm a bit nervous about going with what the person behind the counter tells me. I got burned buying my first laptop that way! My budget maxes out at $10,000. Will I be able to find anything decent at that price? If so, can you point me in the right direction?

Thanks so much—and don't forget to let me know the next time you need golf gear.

Best,

A Favor from Your Supervisor

Subject: Change in Vacation Schedule

Carl,

At the start of the year, I said I'd be on vacation for the two weeks beginning on September 12 and ending on September 23.

I just received an invitation to join my cousins, who will be visiting Italy from October 15 to October 26. One of them can't make it, and the ticket is nonrefundable, so they are giving it to me.

I know it is short notice, and an exception to company policy, but if there is any way you can agree, I would be so grateful. If you find yourself understaffed during the holidays, I'll be happy to pitch in and work between Christmas and New Year.

Thank you for your consideration.

FOLLOW-UPS

Sometimes it's a good idea to send a reminder of a request before its due date. Sometimes a request really did get inadvertently buried on someone's desk; sometimes the recipient has buried it on purpose, hoping it will disappear or you will ask someone else. A reminder can help achieve the desired result before it's too late.

Request for Performance Reviews

Performance reviews can be time consuming and, when treated with appropriate seriousness, can be difficult, but they are necessary. Many things—raises, promotions, and remediation plans—flow from them.

Subject: Reminder: Performance Evaluations Are Due

I have received performance reviews from about half the managers. They will give me a jumpstart on the process. Thank you.

If you have not yet turned in your team's reviews, remember that they are due on the 29th. As you know, salary and promotion discussions are scheduled for the week of December 5. Individual discussions with managers about performance issues will also be held that week. Obviously, we cannot proceed without the reviews, and delays will cause problems for the HR managers as well as the payroll department.

Thank you for your cooperation.

When There Has Been No Response to a Proposal

Direct communication—in person or on the phone—is the first step toward following up when you have had no response to a proposal. The recipient may be interested, but swamped. Or she may be ducking your calls because she is not interested, or because she is having difficulty telling you that there is a problem with it. But you won't know until you make contact. You can help by giving her a way to get past the hurdle.

> Subject: Proposal for Office Remodeling
>
> Dear Kate,
>
> I know you are busy and have been traveling, and I know how crazy things can be when you return to the office. I assume that's why I keep missing you when I call.
>
> I don't want to add to the pressure you already are under, but I wondered if you'd had a chance to look at the proposal I sent. If you are swamped, and haven't had a chance, I'll understand. We can talk when you have cleared your desk a bit. If you have questions about any aspect of it—I know you weren't certain what you wanted to see happen with the new cafeteria—let's discuss it. We'll be happy to make modifications.
>
> Could you give me a quick call or drop me an e-mail to let me know how you want to proceed? Thank you.

CHAPTER FOURTEEN

Thank You

Showing You Care

The list of things you can thank people for is infinite. In earlier chapters, we have already shown you how to thank people for many things; we suspect that more letters begin and end with thanking the recipient than any other thing.

SIMPLY STATED

Business thank-you notes

- may be brief
- may be handwritten or word processed
- may be a card, a letter, or an e-mail, but *not* a memo
- should be sent promptly
- should be sincere
- should be personal

In this chapter, we'll take a look at the many ways to say *thank you*, and the many things you might thank people for in business situations.

Thank-you notes are always nicest when they are handwritten (assuming your handwriting is legible—many people's isn't). Handwritten notes just seem to take more effort and feel that much more personal. Typed letters, even e-mails, are acceptable. The most important thing is to say it—you'd be surprised at how many people forget to do it—and, although manners are increasingly informal, people do notice when their efforts go unacknowledged.

You should write a thank-you note to acknowledge

- a favor
- an introduction
- a gift
- a business lunch or dinner
- a meeting
- an assignment or freelance employment
- and myriad other events.

THANK-YOU NOTES FOR EVERY OCCASION

A Favor

Subject: Thanks so much for lending a hand

Jonah,

Thanks so much for staying late the night before the exhibit opened to help me set up the booth! When the shipping company left our shipment in Honolulu instead of delivering to the exhibit center in Oahu, I thought we'd had it. When it did arrive at 9 o'clock, I thought I'd have to pull an all-nighter to get it set up. Your help saved the day (or should I say night?)! I couldn't have done it without you.

An Introduction

Dear Liz,

I can't thank you enough for introducing me to Charles Wainwright. He was the perfect guide through the maze of government environmental protection regulations. Little did we anticipate, when we bought this property way back when, that when we wanted to update and renovate and bring it into the twenty-first century, we'd discover the environmental sinkhole it had become.

Charles was able to introduce us to the right team of environmental specialists, including engineers, contractors, and architects, so that we were able to make the improvements in compliance with current regulations with the least discombobulation. He was a lifesaver and I have you to thank (my boss thinks I am a miracle worker!).

I hope that one day I'll be able to return the favor; please call on me whenever you need anything.

Best,

A Gift

Dear Spike,

Wherever did you find that fantastic antique desk set? It looks perfect in our new showroom—so elegant. I can't tell you how many clients have asked me where they can buy one. Of course, it is unique, so I have to tell them they can't. It's truly lovely!

Thank you so much.

A Business Lunch or Dinner

Subject: Dinner

I so enjoyed seeing you last night. Dinner was scrumptious. I'd never been to La Dolce Vita before; people had told me it was fabulous, so when you suggested it I was looking forward to it, but it was even better than I expected.

In addition to good food and company, I always learn so much whenever we meet. Please do send me the script for John's new show. It could be something we'd be interested in backing.

An Order

Dear Mr. Konrad,

Thank you for allowing me to present the Stone Cold File Storage System to you and the rest of the operations team at Hardwick Financial. Please pass along special thanks to Lily and Peter for setting everything up so efficiently.

In the financial industry, perhaps more than any other, the importance of preserving hard copy documents as well as electronic backup media cannot be underestimated. Recent natural disasters, such as hurricanes, have brought this lesson home to many of us.

As we discussed, your present system, while excellent when it was first implemented fifteen years ago, is no longer state of the art. I know you were concerned about the disruption that might result if you had to start from scratch, but, because it was such a good system, we can bring it up to date without any downtime. I have consulted with our technicians and we are preparing a detailed proposal, which I will send to you next week, that will explain the specifics of how this can be implemented. It should, I believe, meet the requirements you and your team outlined.

Once you have had a chance to review our proposal, I suggest that we meet again the week of the 17th to discuss any questions you might have as well as the logistics involved in getting started.

We look forward to working with you and helping you build a new state-of-the-art storage facility that will provide a model for the industry.

Very truly yours,

An Assignment or Freelance Employment

Subject: Birds of Prey

Carrie,

Thank you so much for the assignment. What nature photographer wouldn't give his eyeteeth to retrace the steps of Audubon and create a photographic parallel of his masterwork?

I will begin shooting on the 21st and, weather permitting, should be back in the studio supervising the printing and selection of the images in about three months, more than ample time to meet your deadline of a rough cut in September.

Thank you so much for this fabulous opportunity.

Appendix

Say What You Mean; Mean What You Say

When you use words incorrectly, or load up your correspondence with junk words and expressions—jargon, euphemisms, and clichés, it detracts from what you have to say. In this appendix we alert you to some of the most common of these pitfalls.

FREQUENTLY CONFUSED AND MISUSED WORDS

Some words are confusing because they sound alike but their meaning is different; other words are misused because their meaning is similar, but not identical. Occasionally, as with *affect* and *effect*, the words not only sound alike, but the difference in their meaning is subtle.

Here are some of the most common causes of error, with examples illustrating how to use them correctly.

accept (verb) to receive

> I *accept* your invitation to lunch.

except (preposition) other than

> *Except* for John, everyone is coming to lunch.

DID YOU KNOW?

The verb *except* is not often used; it means to *leave out*, to *take out*, or to *omit*.

> You *except* the women from the meeting, which is sexist.

The word *exception* comes from the same root.

advice (noun) an opinion or suggestion as to what should be done

If she had taken my *advice*, she would have accepted the job offer.

advise (verb) to recommend, notify, or inform

I *advise* you to accept the job offer.

affect (verb) to influence

Do not let the loss of one account *affect* your enthusiasm.

effect (noun) a result

The loss of the account did not have an *effect* on me.

effect (verb) to bring about

I can *effect* a change on morale by hosting a holiday party.

all (collective noun)—requires a plural verb

All of us are going to the trade fair in Los Angeles in May.

each (singular noun)—requires a singular verb

Each of us is going to pack for the trip tomorrow evening.

among (preposition) refers to the relationship of three or more—never just two—things.

We have to choose *among* 17 applicants for the job.

between (preposition) refers to the relationship of two—never more—things.

It came down to a choice *between* Jake Johanssen and Myra Breckenridge.

amount (noun) sum, total—used with mass or things that are unable to be counted

The *amount* of energy consumed by time spent on the phone is incalculable.

number (noun) the sum total of people or things—used when referring to things that can be counted

The *number* of phone calls made by the Eastern Division outpaced those of all other districts combined.

bad (adjective)—used to describe nouns

> John had a *bad* cold, so I had to make the presentation for him.

badly (adverb)—used to modify verbs

> Cynthia performed *badly* on her CPA exam and will have to take it again.

Did You Know?

There's an important exception to this rule: With verbs like *feel* and *look*, use *bad* to describe someone's appearance; *badly* could be used with these verbs to describe a lack of physical sensation.

> John's cold made him look *bad* as well as feel *bad*.

He feels *badly* as a result of his accident, which left him with no sensation in his fingers.

can (verb) be able to—indicates certainty

> He *can* close the deal; he's on his game.

may (verb) might be able to—indicates possibility

> He *may* close the deal, if he's on his game.

will/shall (verbs)—indicate certainty about a future action

> He *will* attend the meeting on Friday and take the minutes.
>
> She *shall* be there at 4 o'clock.

Will and shall may be used interchangeably.

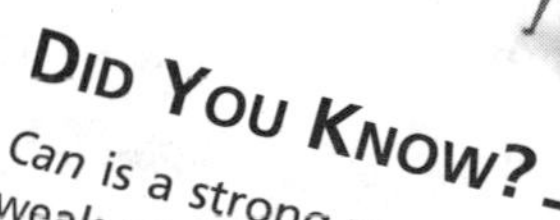

Did You Know?

Can is a strong word; *may* is a weak word. When choosing a word, consider the message you want to convey.

could/would (verbs)—express possibility, but some doubt about an action

> He *could* attend the meeting on Friday and take the minutes if he were asked.
>
> He *would* attend the meeting on Friday and take the minutes if he were asked.

due to (phrase) as a result of—modifies nouns; most often used after some form of the verb *to be*

> Earl's success is *due to* a combination of brilliance and perseverance.

because of (phrase) as a result of—used to modify verbs

Virginia left the strategy team *because of* her lack of enthusiasm for the project.

When in doubt, choose *because of*—it's rarely incorrect. One more thing, *never* say *due to the fact that*, which merely adds unnecessary words, or *the reason is because*, which is redundant. You could say *the reason is that*, but why bother when *because* says it all?

compare with (phrase)—used when discussing similar things

When I compare the sales of Brown & Co with those of Oppenheimer & Co., I learn a great deal.

compare to (phrase)—used when discussing different things

When I compare the number of suicides in Sweden to the weather in New York, I learn nothing, although it does prove a point about statistics.

complement (verb) to make complete

To *complement* the report, I am going to commission some new graphs.

complement (noun) something that completes

We now have a full *complement* of sales reps out in the field.

compliment (verb) to congratulate

I must *compliment* you on the informative talk you gave this morning.

compliment (noun) something said in praise.

Thank you for the *compliment*.

comprise (verb) to be made up of, to include, to contain, to consist of—used only when referring to an entire thing

The organization is *comprised* of 20 divisions.

consist of (verb) to be formed of, to be composed of

You may not say, *20 divisions comprise the organization*, but you can say, *the organization consists of 20 divisions*.

When in doubt, use consist; you'll be just fine.

consensus (noun) opinion held by most or all; general agreement—takes a singular verb

The *consensus* is that we should move the office to Florida.

Consensus of opinion is redundant.

continual (adjective) repeated often

Continual reinforcement of the benefit of the gadget will make it the buyer's first choice.

continuous (adjective) going on without interruption

Our company has been in *continuous* operation for over 150 years.

data (noun) facts, statistics, evidence—plural of Latin *datum*; takes a plural verb

The *data show* that this should be a good year for growth stocks.

data (collective noun) a single collection of information—takes a singular verb.

The *data is* available for viewing in the treasurer's office.

In business, either a singular or a plural verb is acceptable.

e.g. (abbreviation) Latin *exempli gratia*; for example, such as

When our competition, *e.g.*, Sal's Suits and T&G Tailors, make presentations, they always let the customer keep the samples.

i.e. (abbreviation) Latin *id est*; that is

When we reach our destination, *i.e.*, sales of $50 million, we will be the largest distributor in the country.

To avoid mistakes, stick to English in business writing.

Did You Know?

When it comes to geography, the distance between further and farther is closing; according some sources, it has closed. Some language mavens say you can use the words interchangeably when referring to distance. What you may not do is use farther as an adverb to mean additional or moreover, and so on.

To take our talk one step *further*, I've asked my staff to provide input.

farther (adjective) more distant or remote

Let's aim for the *farther* goal.

farther (adverb) at or to a greater physical distance or a more remote point

The *farther* my office is from my boss's office, the less I see him.

further (adverb) additional, more, moreover; to the greatest degree or extent

He took the idea *further* than anyone else on staff had, and created a best-selling ad campaign.

fewer (adjective) a smaller number

We absorbed *fewer* losses during the storm than our competition did.

less (adjective) smaller in size or amount

The *less* work and the more play, the happier some people are.

first/last (noun)—use these when more than two items are mentioned

Mint, melon, and peach were the colors chosen for the new packaging. The *first* was chosen for the label; the *last* was chosen for the ribbon.

former/latter (noun)—use this pair when only two items are mentioned

One computer's list price is $795; the other's is $1,050. Dell manufactures the *former*, Hewlett Packard the *latter*.

foreword (noun) an introductory statement about a book written by someone other than the author

> I was flattered that Josephine March agreed to write the *foreword* to my new book.

forward (adverb) toward or at a place, point, or time in advance

> As we move the campaign *forward*, we will have to make certain we do not overspend.

Most people understand the different meanings of these two words, but *foreword* is frequently misspelled. If you remember that a *foreword* comes *before* the author's words, you may never confuse the spelling again.

good (adjective) effective, beneficial—used to describe a noun

> It was a very *good* meeting; we learned a great deal about the new product.

well (adverb) in a good manner—used to provide information about a verb

> The meeting went *well*; the speaker provided a great deal of information.

imply (verb) to hint, to intimate, to allude

> I don't mean to *imply* he cheated, but his grades improved dramatically.

infer (verb) to draw a conclusion, to derive

> Am I to *infer* from what you said that John is going to be promoted?

insure (verb) to guarantee against harm or loss

> I am going to *insure* the new office for full replacement value.

ensure (verb) to guarantee, to make certain, to make safe

> I am going *ensure* that each employee is driven home from the holiday party.

assure (verb) to guarantee (a dubious) thing

I can *assure* you that we will get that contract tomorrow.

it's (contraction) it is

It's going to be difficult meeting our goals this quarter.

its (pronoun) indicates ownership

Each cubicle will come equipped with *its* own recycling bin.

lay/set/raise (verbs) all describe things a person (or any noun) does *to* something, including oneself

If you *lay* the books down, you'll be able to stretch.

I *set* myself down for a long meeting.

I *raise* a glass of champagne to toast all of you for a job well done.

lie/sit/rise (verbs) all describe things a person *does*

After a long day's work, I *lie* down and sleep like a log.

I *sit* upright so that my back won't hurt during a long meeting.

I *rise* at dawn to get into the office by 7:30.

Many of these words have other meetings and forms—too many to discuss here—but this is where the confusion lies (*not* lays).

may be (verb) is possible

It *may be* that we will get the assignment; the feedback is positive.

maybe (adverb) possibly

Maybe the advertising agency will give us the assignment.

ones (noun) plural of the number one (1)

I market tested the new candy; the *ones* with the caramel centers were least popular.

one's (possessive pronoun)

oneself (reflexive pronoun)

One could hurt *oneself* badly, at least in terms of *one's* career, if one disagreed with the boss too often.

DID YOU KNOW?

Although one, one's, and *oneself* were losing ground for many years—too formal and stuffy—they (especially one's) are making a comeback as writers try to use gender-neutral language.

past (adverb) beyond

Martha drives *past* my house every morning on her way to work.

past (noun) bygone

In the *past*, the company hosted an annual party at the convention, but the costs are prohibitive today.

passed (verb) past tense of *to pass*

Harry *passed* Bruce and became the number one sales rep in just a few months.

principal (adjective) main, primary

principal (noun) a person who is first in rank or importance; the head of a school

The *principal* speaker at the convention was Marva Connaught, who is also a *principal* in Stein, Connaught, Hastings.

principal (noun) in finance, the amount of money on which interest is computed

He invested his *principal* wisely, and, on average, earned 12% a year.

principle (noun) the source of something; a fundamental truth, doctrine, or law; integrity

The *principle* on which my father built this company is to provide the highest quality possible.

regard (noun) consideration, attention, relating to, respect, affections

I hold Peter Tanous in the highest *regard*.

In *regard* to your letter of the June 26, we have made the adjustment you requested.

regards (noun) respect, affection, best wishes; frequently used in salutations

Please give Peter Tanous my best *regards* when you see him.

As *regards* your letter of June 26, we have made the adjustment you requested.

Using the word *regards* is correct, but never use *in regards*. To avoid errors, unless you are giving best wishes to someone, use *regard*.

stationary (adjective) standing still

Please remain *stationary* until the machine has stopped.

stationery (noun) paper, envelopes, and other writing material

When the company moved, we had to purchase new *stationery*.

than (conjunction) in comparison with

Wal-Mart is bigger *than* its competitors.

then (adverb) soon after, next

Then we introduced the new model, and our sales increased by 200%.

then (adjective) at that time

The *then* director of operations saved the company a fortune by renovating the warehouse.

their (possessive pronoun) belonging to them

Their company increased its annual revenues every year for five years.

there (adverb) at that place

There is nowhere to go but up after the losses we've taken this year.

they're (contraction) they are

They're going to be happy when they see the sales forecast.

to (preposition) in the direction of

He went *to* Wharton for his MBA.

too (adverb) also, in addition

She, *too*, went to Wharton.

two (adjective) a cardinal number

Two of my colleagues attended Wharton for the MBAs.

your (possessive pronoun) belonging to you

you're (contraction) you are

If *you're* going to make a presentation, give it *your* best shot.

JARGON, CLICHES, AND EUPHEMISMS TO AVOID

Some language is so overused, obfuscatory, or unclear that it detracts from your writing. Examine your writing with an eye toward avoid jargon, clichés, and euphemisms, except in their appropriate context. A *cliché* is a trite or overused expression or idea. *Jargon** refers to specialized words and phrases, often found in business writing, that are essentially unintelligible to outsiders, or even meaningless in themselves. Writers sometimes use jargon to aggrandize themselves or their group, but the technique often backfires, annoying readers who are not members of the club. A *euphemism* is the substitution of a mild, indirect, or vague expression for one considered to be offensive, harsh, or blunt; for example, *consolidation* instead of *layoff*.

The following is a selected list of words and phrases to avoid in your writing.

accommodate concerns
actionable
aggressive quote
ambush marketing
architect (used as a verb)
arrows to fire
at the end of the day
at some juncture
Band-Aid
bandwidth (in its nontechnical sense)
believe in
benchmark
benign report
best of breed
best practices
boots on the ground
bottom line
bounce [an idea] off someone
brings a lot of value to the table
bring our "A" game
bring them along
brushfire
bullish on
business case
buy in

*We are not talking here about words that are specific to a particular trade, profession, or group; for example, medical, legal, or technical jargon, which has a place in correspondence among members of that group. If used outside the group—for example, when no other word is possible—it should be explained in lay terms.

calm market
cash burn rate
cash flow benefits
cast a wider net
challenges
check [someone's] temperature
circle back/circle back around
clamp down
client-centered
commitment
compelling case
confidence in the future
consolidation
core competency
cost containment
cost management
create value
crisis management
corporate culture
customer is always right, the
customizable
data driven
disintermediation
don't throw out the baby with the bathwater
down game changing
down integrated approach
downscaleable
down size or downsize
down viral
drink the Kool-Aid
drill down
drive [a point] home
drop the ball
dynamic
80%-20% rule, the
eat our own dog food
eco-[anything]
elephant in the room (or the corner), the
engineered solutions
faster, cheaper, better
feeding the hopper
financial drag
focused on
follow up on
from a . . . standpoint
game changer
get a good start [a jump] on
get a handle on
given a mandate
giving 110%
go a long way toward
good to go
going forward
going from good to great
granularity
hard spot
has legs and can go really far
high performance
hired gun
honestly
I appreciate your candor
if we have the courage of our convictions
I'll sharpen the pencil
impactful
improve ROI
in depth
industry leader
insourced
in the . . . space
integrated marketing
intelligent engineering
interact with
in terms of

internal efficiencies
in today's highly competitive marketplace . . .
in the trenches with you . . .
it is what it is
is hot
issues
lead dog
leading provider of
leaner
let's be proactive here, people
let's get granular
let's hit the ground running
let's take this offline
leverage
like a . . . on steroids
long haul
long term
loss leader
low-hanging fruit
major player
manage expectations
marketing-driven
matrix management
maximize customer satisfaction
maximize leverage
milestone
monetize
more competitive
moving up the value chain
multitask
my way or the highway
net-net
new and improved
next generation
noise in the system
1+1=3
offline
off-ramp
on target
on-ramp
opportunity
organic growth
our go-to-market strategy
our people are our best asset
out-of-pocket
outsource
paradigm
paradigm shift
pare down
partner with
perfect storm
ping
play a role
plug-and-play
plus for all stakeholders, a
position a product
precision-engineered
proactive
pull-through sales
purple cow
push the envelope
put a stake in the ground
quality is job one
quite frankly
raise the bar
ramping down [an operation]
reinvented
reorganization
restructuring
right size or rightsize
rigor
rising tide raises all boats
robust
robust and customer-focused
rubber hits the road

run it up the flagpole and see who salutes
sacrifice
scalability
scenery only changes for the lead dog, the
seamless integration
shelved
showstopper
situation
skate to where the puck is going
spending more time with my family
spin
strategic
stay abreast
stick a fork in it . . . it's done
surplused
suspend operations
sustainability
switching gears
synergy
24/7
take it to the next level
team player
teamwork
tearing down the silos
termination
think outside of the box
thought leader
today, more than ever
top line
touch base
trim costs
trim fat
under the radar
up sell
up to the plate
user-experience
user-focused
value added
value-added proposition
viable
way forward, the
well positioned
we'll loop you in
whatever it takes
win-win
win-win situation
your take

Glossary

Words and Phrases Commonly Used in Business

account	a customer or client; also a bookkeeping entry
advance	partial amount paid on a contract, often prior to the beginning of work, sometimes at various points stipulated in an agreement
agreement	agreement between or among parties to do something in return for specified services and compensation; less formal than a contract, but usually results in a contract
balance	difference between debits and credits, may be positive or negative; may also refer to the amount of money in an account or the amount of money owed to a creditor
boilerplate	standard language that appears in every contract or agreement; often a preprinted form
cash flow	actual amount of money paid and received in a given period of time; may be positive or negative
COD	(cash on delivery) full amount or balance due that completes payment
collateral	some tangible asset—for example, stock, bonds, or real estate—used to secure a loan
compensation	salary, benefits, or other things of value given to an employee in exchange for work performed
confidential	information held privately; should not be disclosed without the other party's permission

confidentiality the obligation to keep something secret; for example, a confidentiality agreement between employer and employee

consideration an amount paid in exchange for a contractual service; binds the parties to the contract; without it a contract is not valid

contract a formal document between or among parties to do something in return for specified services and compensation

counteroffer in negotiations, response to an offer with another offer; may apply to salary, benefits, due dates, or other terms in an agreement

credit in accounting, to enter a payment, or the entry itself, in an account

credit rating formal evaluation of a person or company's ability to pay

credit standing similar to credit rating, a person's or company's reputation for reliably making payments

debit in accounting, to enter an expense, or the entry itself, in an account

debt amount owed

discount list price less a stipulated dollar amount or percentage that reduces the selling price of goods or services; discount may also be given for prompt payment of an invoice

dun to request payment of a debt

equity amount of ownership based on the amount of money still owed, for example, on a major piece of equipment or real estate

franchise a license or right to operate a business; may be granted by a government or a corporation; for example a McDonald's franchise

good faith payment partial payment of a debt to demonstrate willingness to meet obligation

goodwill a positive relationship with customers and vendors; in accounting, an intangible asset, for example, a brand name that has value

inventory property or merchandise in a company's possession

invoice an itemized bill, showing price(s), total charge, and terms

libel	legally, anything written or printed that is defamatory or that maliciously misrepresents; colloquially, used interchangeably with slander
list price	original price on an item as listed in the catalog
net	amount after all discounts, deductions, expenses, and so on
offer	an indication of interest
progress payment	similar to an advance; payment made based on performance of stipulated work; frequently used in construction
proposal	a business plan that is proposed
prospect	potential customer or client
RFP	request for proposal; formal solicitation of a proposal to perform specific work
SASE	self-addressed stamped envelope; most used by direct mail advertisers but also by others wishing to encourage response; for example, charitable organizations, conductors of surveys
slander	legally, anything said orally that is defamatory or that maliciously misrepresents; colloquially, used interchangeably with libel
terms	items stipulated in a contract; for example, how much is to be paid, when payment is to be made, and under what conditions
tickler file	a file of memoranda or notices that remind of things to be done
2/10 net 30	on an invoice, indicates that if full payment is made within 10 days, the customer may take a 2% discount; otherwise the total amount is due within 30 days